BIBLICAL GROUNDS:

A Christian Guide to Divorce

Ray McBerry

Copyright (c) 2023 by Landmark Heritage Press

All rights reserved.

No part of this book may be reproduced, distributed or transmitted in any form or by any means, including photocopying, recording, or other electronic or mechanical methods, without the prior written permission of the publisher, except in the case of brief quotations embodied in critical reviews and certain other non-commercial uses permitted by copyright law.

All of the case studies presented in this book are based upon actual events, but all of the names have been changed.

All Scripture is taken from the Authorized King James Version.

Forward and Dedication

This is a book that had to be written. As an author, I have a stack of other books which were already on my "to write" list. But as a pastor, after much prayer, I've come to the conclusion that this one has to be written next. This book contains the many things about this important subject that I discovered while studying the Bible for itself. It contains many things that I never heard growing up in good, Bible-believing churches; and it contains many things that I was never even taught in Bible college or seminary. In the defense of the pastors and Bible college teachers that I mimicked, I'm sure that they were merely doing the same in mimicking those who had taught them before, just as I did. But there are thousands upon thousands of people who sincerely love God and desperately want to know and do His will in their lives who have been misled, even if unwittingly by their pastors and teachers, about the subject of divorce; and their consciences are wrongly convicted because of inadequate teaching on what the Bible says. There are both men and women who are staying in marriages out of a misinformed feeling of guilt but have legitimate Biblical grounds for divorce. Likewise, there are all too many couples seeking divorce as a solution to their marital problems who lack any Biblical grounds whatsoever for a divorce. This book is dedicated to a close friend who struggled for too long with the subject of divorce because of a sincere desire to please God while already having Biblical grounds.

Table of Contents

Part 1: Why the need for this book? 7

Part 2: The Covenantal Nature of Marriage 13

    God-ordained Institutions................................14

    The Institution of Marriage 15

    Marriage as a Covenant 18

    Marriage Vows..21

    Marriage Licenses 25

    The Act of Marriage 27

    Roles in Marriage...29

    Biblical Admonitions to Husbands and Wives......30

    God's Order in the Home 33

    Decision-making in Marriage 37

    Conclusion on Marriage.................................40

Part 3: Divorce 41

    The Necessity of Divorce................................43

    The Breaking of the Marriage Covenant..........45

Part 4: What are the Biblical Grounds?................51

    An Introduction to this Chapter 51

    Are Old Testament Biblical Grounds Still In Effect Today?.....52

    A Final Plea to Read the Previous Chapters ...56

    Biblical Ground #1: Adultery 57

Biblical Ground #2: Physical Abandonment 63

Biblical Ground #3: Leaving and Cleaving 70

Biblical Ground #4: Constructive Abandonment 87

Biblical Ground #5: Financial Slavery 94

Biblical Ground #6: Having no Delight In 98

Biblical Ground #7: Withholding the Act of Marriage 102

Biblical Ground #8: Fraud 108

Biblical Ground #9: Abuse 127

Biblical Ground #10: Dealing Treacherously 138

Biblical Grounds: Summary 142

PART 5: I Have Biblical Grounds for Divorce. Now What? . 143

Divorce or Reconciliation 144

Forgiveness and Staying 148

The Right Process for Ending Your Marriage 152

When is it Officially Over? 155

Appendices 157

One more clarification of Matthew 19:9 157

Two times that divorce is explicitly prohibited in the Bible. .. 159

Divorce and remarriage 161

Divorce and Qualifications of a Pastor 164

Part 1

Why the need for this book?

As a pastor, I sat across a table in our church fellowship hall from a dear lady in our church who only a couple of hours earlier had told her husband that she was leaving him. He had called me, frantic, and at first asked me to meet him at the church immediately. At first, I did not know what his reason was for wanting to meet so abruptly; but it seemed like an obvious emergency, so I dropped what I was doing and headed straight to the church.

I did not know the man very well. His wife and children had attended our church faithfully for about three years since they had joined the church; but he rarely attended, himself. He was waiting for me in the parking lot when I pulled up at the church and followed me inside the fellowship hall. The man explained that he had just had a long argument with his wife and that she had told him that she was leaving him. The next words out of his mouth went something like this: "Preacher, tell her that she has to stay because the Bible says she has to." He then followed it up with some other things that included, "She can't go. Neither of us can make it on our own financially; I won't be able to pay the bills. And I won't ever be able to find anybody else." He then added that he loved her and didn't want her to go.

As a pastor, you eventually get used to hearing all sorts of things when counseling both members and non-members in your flock; but even as a pastor, hearing him list the first two reasons out of his mouth that he did not want her to leave was cringe worthy. Yes, he had added that he loved her; but I distinctly remember the feeling that I had in the pit of my stomach when the first two reasons out of his mouth were related to him being able to pay the bills and him being able to find someone else. I am fairly certain that this would have sent up red flags for even most unbelievers who lacked any sort of spiritual discernment; but the fact that those two concerns came out of his mouth instead of "I love her and can't imagine life without her" (or something to that effect) was very telling.

After spending another half hour or so speaking to him and asking him questions, the man admitted a number of things that he had done and was still doing wrong in the marriage. He even went so far as to say something along the lines of "It's all my fault, preacher. I know it's all my fault. She's been telling me these things for years and asking me to change." Over the course of the next year, he admitted additional things to me from time to time that he had failed to tell me during our initial meeting; but, still, the things that he did admit were certainly not in keeping with the way that the New Testament says that a husband should treat his wife. Nevertheless, when I questioned him repeatedly as to whether he had committed infidelity of any kind, he consistently said, "No."

I agreed to speak to his wife if she was willing; and about an hour after he left, she arrived. To her credit, she did not attempt to list all of his sins and indiscretions; in fact, she was reluctant to even acknowledge them when I recounted the list that he had given me, himself, of his wrongdoings in the marriage. Ultimately, I asked her whether she had reason to believe that he had been unfaithful; and, with a relatively long pause, she replied that there was nothing that she could prove.

As a very conservative Baptist preacher – and someone who has tried sincerely during my entire life to base every thing that I believe upon the Word of God – I did what any preacher would do in that situation... I explained to the best of my knowledge what the Bible said about divorce and showed her the passages in black and white. Calling upon everything that I had been taught in Bible college and the few times growing up that I had heard messages preached on divorce, I told her that there were really only two Biblical reasons for a Christian to consider leaving a marriage... adultery or abandonment by the other party as an unbeliever.

I remember distinctly as this dear lady began sobbing uncontrollably as she said, "Why would God do that to me? Why would He allow me to be mistreated like this?" This was a lady that I watched walk with the Lord for the entire three or so years that they had attended our church. She was faithful to every service, volunteered for anything that needed to be done at church from helping with the kids in the church to cleaning the toilets and mopping the floors. She listened attentively to the teaching and preaching and frequently asked questions. But more than that, I had seen her repeatedly go out of her way to live out her faith in witnessing to others and offering to do things for others even when no one else knew. To the best of my ability to see as a pastor, this was a sincere, Godly lady who was trying to serve the Lord.

Without being conscious of it, this dear lady was saying, "I know our God too well to know that He is not okay with me being treated this way. He would never allow His daughter to be treated like I've been treated by any man." And she was right. She instinctively knew from the many years of reading her Bible and faithfully listening to preaching both at our church and those that she had attended previously that even though our God is a holy God with very clearly stated views on marriage and divorce, He is also a caring, loving, protective Father who watches over His children and deplores the mistreatment of the innocent. She knew, despite what her sincere pastor was telling her, that it was inconsistent with Who our God is to believe that He would require her to remain in the situation in which she found herself at that moment.

Eventually, though, after another hour or so of talking and praying, this dear lady agreed to go back home and give her husband "another chance" instead of finally leaving. I sincerely believed that I had counselled her Biblically, and I was greatly relieved that she had agreed to remain in her marriage. Still, though, the initial words out of her husband's mouth when I first met with him – coupled with the many wrongs that he had admitted to me, himself – left a bitter taste in my own mouth. Then, within a month's time, I witnessed the husband's commitment to weekly counseling dwindle away and disappear, along with most of the other promises that he had made privately to her, the preacher, and, I suppose, to God.

Over the course of the next year, there were multiple other occasions when the same husband came to me again and confessed additional sins and wrongdoings on his own part in their marriage that he had not previously revealed to me. Each time the list of evils seemed to pile up higher and higher than what I had been told before... but they never included adultery; and for that one reason alone, I continued to counsel her to stay in the marriage each time that he ended his voluntary "confession" to me by saying, "Preacher, you've got to tell her that she has to stay. I haven't committed adultery."

I finally did what I should have done long ago; it is the same thing that I have prided myself on in both my private life and my ministry for my entire life... I dug into the Word of God to see what it said for myself. I had done this for countless other subjects whenever I or one of my church members has had a question about spiritual things over the years. Why had I not done it long before then regarding the important subject of divorce? I certainly had counseled many individuals about marriage and divorce over the years; but it was not until this particular situation and the injustice that seemed to accompany it that I felt compelled to look into the Word of God to see if what I had been taught in Bible college and in Sunday School classes my whole life was correct. I felt sure that it was. After all, I had grown up in church all my life and had been to Bible college. I even had my post-graduate degree in Bible hanging on the wall.

After digging into the Word for several long months on the subject of divorce, I remember the day that that particular husband came to me again out of the blue to make one of his voluntary "confessions" like he had done on multiple occasions over that past year. He again shared yet one more thing that I had not known previously and then said as he had become accustomed to saying when he finished each time, "Preacher, tell her she has to stay. It's not like I've committed adultery." You could have heard a pin drop when this time I replied, "No, I'm not going to tell her that anymore. I think she has Biblical grounds for divorce, and it's between her and God if she stays or goes." All of a sudden he no longer wanted the pastor counseling his wife, and he abruptly ordered me not to tell her what I had just told him. I smiled and said, "That's not the way it works. If she comes to me, I'll show her what the Bible says so that she can see it for herself; and it will be between her and the Lord what she does." From that day on, that man had no more use for the preacher who wouldn't continue to do his bidding.

When I was asked, I shared with that dear lady what I had learned from studying the Bible for myself instead of taking the word of those who had taught me growing up. I have spent many times since in tears over the realization that my inadequate counseling was the reason that a Godly lady who trusted her pastor remained in an unjust situation for another year of torment when all along she intuitively knew from her understanding of our God that – even though she didn't yet know chapter or verse to support it – He is not a God who would require one of His children to remain in an unjust situation.

It is essential that the Word of God be the final authority on questions of divorce, just as it should be in all other questions of life. All other "authorities" are arbitrary and subject to change, whether they be the thoughts of the greatest philosophers of the day, the teachings of the current popular preachers, or even the laws of your state. All of these, even at their best, are but the musings of man with his finite intellect, emotion, and understanding of things. That is not so of the Word of God; it is absolute, pure, holy, and proceeds directly from the mind and heart of God to man. It is the Word of God by which we will all be judged one day; and, so, therefore, it should be the authority by which we measure all of our decisions and actions. And because it emanates from God, Himself, we can rest assured that it will not mislead us and that, in spite of whatever men may say contrary to its teachings, its advice for us contains what is best for us. Thus is the reason that any justification for divorce must necessarily, for both conscience's sake and for practicality's sake, be rooted in Biblical grounds.

It is my hope that this book serves not so much as a justification for divorce as it does as a reminder to us all of the sanctity of marriage in the eyes of a holy God; and that, in turn, it may lead even those heretofore guilty back into an understanding of what He expects and may, thereby, save those marriages which are worth saving. And for those who have suffered injustice, I pray that it will relieve their consciences to discover that they, too, may have Biblical grounds for divorce even when adultery and abandonment are not present. May this book be used to save lives, homes, consciences, and souls.

Part 2

The Covenantal Nature of Marriage

It is impossible to have a good understanding of the Biblical grounds for divorce without a deep understanding of and appreciation for the Biblical view of marriage, itself; for the Biblical grounds for divorce are all predicated upon a violation of one or more violations of the marriage covenant.

To read the following sections of this book without reading this one would create an incomplete understanding of marriage and, thereby, divorce; and it would potentially open the door for some or all of the parts of the next section of this book to be misinterpreted and taken out of proper context... which is exactly what the Bible warns against when we are told to "rightly divide the word of God."

God-ordained Institutions

In the Bible, we have revealed to us the four basic institutions of human existence that are ordained by God. The first of these is the individual. God first created Adam. He later created Eve. Both Adam and Eve, just as you and I today, were given certain rights and responsibilities in their individual capacity. Each individual is created in the image of God; that is, each of us is an eternal soul made of three parts – body, soul, and spirit – and because of this, each of us will exist somewhere eternally. Additionally, when God created man, He bestowed upon him some (but not all) of His sovereignty and dominion over the other parts of creation. Man is to use the sovereignty that God has given him over creation for God's glory and for his use. Mankind also has individual responsibilities, and each of us are obligated by God to fulfill those responsibilities; they are clearly laid out for us in divine Scripture. God has also ordained the church and given it certain dominion and certain responsibilities. So, too, has He ordained civil government and given to it certain dominion and certain responsibilities. And, finally, He has ordained the family and given to it certain responsibilities while circumscribing its dominion in the affairs of men. Each of these four human institutions ordained by God – the individual, the family, the church, and civil government – have their own sphere of authority in our lives (whether we choose to recognize it or not), and each has its own responsibilities that must be maintained.

The Institution of Marriage

Generally speaking, marriage is God's plan for individuals. Genesis 2:18 tells us, *"And the Lord God said, It is not good that the man should be alone; I will make him an help meet for him."* That is not to say that there are not exceptions to this, however. In I Corinthians 7:8, Paul gave the following advice to widows: *"I say therefore to the unmarried and widows, It is good for them if they abide even as I."* And, again, in the same chapter, beginning in verse 27, Paul says to virgins (both men and women), *"Now concerning virgins I have no commandment of the Lord: yet I give my judgment, as one that hath obtained mercy of the Lord to be faithful. I suppose therefore that this is good for the present distress, I say, that it is good for a man so to be. Art thou bound unto a wife? seek not to be loosed. Art thou loosed from a wife? seek not a wife."* In that particular instance, Paul was not giving a commandment from the Lord, as he plainly states, but was giving advice that those in that particular situation (intense persecution of the early church) would be wise to remain unmarried for the present. This would also seem to indicate that there may be other extenuating circumstances even today in which it might be preferable for an individual to remain unmarried for either a season or even permanently. These exceptions aside, however, it is obvious from Scripture that God's overarching plan for mankind involves marriage in every age of history.

Although it may seem obvious to most, perhaps in today's world it is important for us to define "marriage." As Christians, again, we are obligated to define the institution of marriage in the way that the Bible defines it. And – much to the world's chagrin – there is no ambiguity in the Word of God as to the definition of marriage. Marriage is the union of one man, one woman, and God in a sanctified relationship. This precludes two men from marrying or two women from marrying. The Bible is emphatic when it states in Genesis 2:22-24: *"And the rib, which the LORD God had taken from man, made he a woman, and brought her unto the man. And Adam said, This is now bone of my bones, and flesh of my flesh: she shall be called Woman, because she was taken out of Man. Therefore shall a man leave his father and his mother, and shall cleave unto his wife: and they shall be one flesh."* The union includes physical, mental, emotional, and spiritual aspects; and it is "sanctified" because it is "set apart" or "exclusive," excluding all other individuals from being a part in it. This not only means that it prohibits a husband and wife from introducing a third member to their intimate relationship, but it also means that parents, children, friends, and all others are outside the marriage relationship. Even children who are a product of the marriage (or of previous marriages by either spouse) are outside the marriage relationship; they may be inside the "family" relationship, but they are outside the marriage relationship. This is what the Lord meant when He said in Genesis 2:24, *"Therefore shall a man leave his father and his mother, and shall cleave unto his wife: and they shall be one flesh."* And again in Ephesians 5:31 which states, *"For this cause shall a man leave his father and mother, and shall be joined unto his wife, and they two shall be one flesh."* There is, quite literally, no way to separate between a husband and wife, there is no room between them for anyone or anything else to fit because they are literally one. I do not mean to imply that husbands and wives do not allow others to come between them and disrupt marriages, for this happens every day. What I do mean to say is that in God's eyes the union between husband and wife does not allow for anyone or anything – save God, Himself – to exist. This means that, in a marriage, the husband and wife are both obligated to have no greater allegiance to anyone or anything above their spouse except for God, Who is to have the highest allegiance of both and is to reside at the center of the union. It is the entering into the institution of marriage which creates this exclusive relationship before both God and man.

Marriage fills the needs of both husband and wife. These needs include the desire for companionship, someone with whom to share life's journey including the ups and the downs, the joys and the sadness, the vacations and the workload. Genesis 2:18 says, *"And the LORD God said, It is not good that the man should be alone; I will make him an help meet for him."* It also fills the need that both have for physical intimacy. The Apostle Paul specifically addressed this in I Corinthians 7:2-4 which states: *"...to avoid fornication, let every man have his own wife, and let every woman have her own husband. Let the husband render unto the wife due benevolence: and likewise also the wife unto the husband. The wife hath not power of her own body, but the husband: and likewise also the husband hath not power of his own body, but the wife."* Marriage is also the vehicle by which God ordained that man should populate the earth. To be sure, He could have simply created every person that has ever lived directly from the earth, Himself, as He did with Adam. Instead, though, He chose to involve man in the process of populating and repopulating the earth through the process of procreation. It is called "procreation" because it is man forwarding God's original act of creation; we do not "create" children as in a direct act of creation as God did Adam but, rather, our children are created "out of" the parents. Procreation, though, is not only one of God's gifts to man through the institution of marriage; it is also a command of God through the institution of marriage. In Genesis 1:28, God initiated this command to procreate to Adam and Eve when He said, *"And God blessed them, and God said unto them, Be fruitful, and multiply, and replenish the earth, and subdue it..."* The reader will undoubtedly think of other possible needs which marriage fills for the husband and wife; but they will fall neatly into one of these three areas, I believe.

Marriage as a Covenant

Marriage is a covenantal relationship. A covenantal relationship involves two or more parties who enter into a formal agreement in which there are binding promises which must be performed. Marriage is not the only covenantal relationship in our everyday lives. Some other examples might include homeowner associations, church membership, and even your employment with your employer. Each of these relationships generally includes a formal agreement, usually in writing, in which one or both parties makes promises to perform certain obligations to the other party. In most covenantal relationships, every party makes obligations to the other party or parties involved; however, there are some instances, such as the Abrahamic Covenant in the Bible (Galatians 3:15-18), in which only one party obligates himself to the other by promising to perform something. Scripturally, of course, a marriage is a covenantal relationship in which both husband and wife are bound by specific promises.

What is a covenant? The term "covenant," although not totally foreign to our modern language, is not one that is a part of our usual, everyday vernacular. It is usually reserved for lawyers and businessmen and courts. Another word for "covenant" is "contract." To be specific, the marriage covenant is a legal contract in which the husband and wife have made binding promises to one another and to God. In reality, God is also a party to the contract in that He has made certain promises to husbands and wives, also; and He is honour-bound to keep His promises related to marriage, as well, which He always does. Scripture clearly explains that as the Sovereign who ordained the institution of marriage and in whose authority marriages are created, He is a party to the contract. Mark 10:9 says this, *"What therefore God hath joined together, let not man put asunder."* These binding promises made by husbands and wives are, in the instance of marriage, called vows. It is the voluntary taking of vows by the husband and wife which make them both parties to the contract. This is important since no one may legally be forced into a contract against their will. In legal terms, a contract is unenforceable if it was not entered into voluntarily by someone in possession of an understanding of their action. The taking of marriage vows, then, is a declaration by both husband and wife that they are freely, willingly, and intentionally entering into the institution of marriage with each other – an institution which was ordained ("officially decreed or established") by God. In Galatians 3:15, Paul reminds us that even men acknowledge the Law of Covenants; that is, covenants are contracts which have obligations which must be fulfilled. The verse says, *"Brethren, I speak after the manner of men; Though it be but a man's covenant, yet if it be confirmed, no man disannulleth, or addeth thereto."* Because the marriage covenant is a contract, it is the breach ("breaking") of the contract by one of the parties which abrogates the contract, making it null and void, of no more effect.

Our God is a covenantal God. Scripture records a number of covenants which He has made with mankind including the Adamic Covenant, the Noahic Covenant, the Abrahamic Covenant, the Mosaic Covenant, and the New Covenant. The name which He gave Moses at the burning bush for Himself is also indicative of His covenantal nature. When Moses asked God who he should tell the children of Israel sent him, God responded, "I AM THAT I AM." The use of the present tense form of the verb "to be" here is God's way of stating that He is self-existent and eternal. He depends upon no one else for His existence and, because He is transcendent above the dimension of time, He is always in the present; He is eternal. In Hebrew, the written name "I AM THAT I AM" was spelled simply with four letters – YHWH. These four letters together are referred to as the tetragram (meaning "four letters"). Their pronunciation (although rarely spoken), according to the ancient Hebrews, was "Yahweh" while the Latinized version is our more familiar "Jehovah." The significance of this name is that it is the name for Himself which He gave specifically for those who knew Him personally; it is an intimate, personal name reserved in Scripture solely for use when God is interacting with His covenant people or with His dominion over creation (which knows Him personally, too). This implies that it is His covenant name with believers and, therefore, also emphasizes His recognition of the importance of covenants and how they separate parties within a covenant from everyone else who lies outside the covenant.

Marriage Vows

Jehovah places great importance on the binding promises that create a covenant – these are the promises that we call vows. In fact, in regard to the vows that we make before God, He says this in Ecclesiastes 5:5: *"Better is it that thou shouldest not vow, than that thou shouldest vow and not pay."* This refers both to vows that we make specifically TO God and vows that we make in which we invoke His name in solemnity, binding ourselves to these vows. Such is the case with the vows which accompany the marriage covenant because they are not only made "in front of God and these witnesses" (making Him a legal witness to the covenant), but also because, as the Creator of the institution of marriage Who alone is the authority which governs it, He is automatically a party to the contract as its arbiter. To illustrate the point that God recognizes the seriousness of vows, even when they are made directly between humans, He has given us the story of Jacob and Esau in the Bible. You may remember the story in Genesis of how Esau, upon coming into the camp and believing he was going to perish, literally sold the birthright to which he was entitled to his younger twin brother Jacob for a bowl of pottage – literally a bowl of soup. Despite it being a foolish decision made on a whim by Esau, God refused to annul the promise, the deal, the vow that he had made to his brother for the birthright. Here's what Hebrews 12:16 and 17 tell us, *"Lest there be any fornicator, or profane person, as Esau, who for one morsel of meat sold his birthright. For ye know how that afterward, when he would have inherited the blessing, he was rejected: for he found no place of repentance, though he sought it carefully with tears."* So then, the covenantal God which we serve places great importance upon the vows that we take and the covenants which those vows create.

In some instances, husbands and wives like to write their own vows. Most often brides and grooms write their own vows for their public wedding ceremony because they wish to express publicly their devotion to their soon-to-be wed. Occasionally in this "post-modern" era, some couples may write their own vows because they deplore the values enshrined in most traditional wedding vows – such as the wife promising to "honour and obey" her husband – and they wish to make a public statement as to their own view of what marriage should be. It is true, by the way, that the vows husbands and wives take are important. Wedding vows constitute the "terms of the contract." They are the binding promises which the parties are making to each other when they enter into the contract – the covenant.

It might seem on its face, then, that husbands and wives are free to create whatever terms of the contract that they wish – something especially appealing to the deviant, pagan culture of the society in which we find ourselves today. However, there are always limits to what the terms of any contract can be; and those limits are always set forth by the sovereign power under whose authority the contract is made. If this sounds like lawyer "legalese" speech, it's probably for a good reason: contract law is the basis for much of our system of laws even to this day, at least in the Western tradition. In order for a contract to be enforceable, from a legal perspective, there must be a higher power which recognizes and thereby lends its authority to the legitimacy of a contract. I'm sure that most lawyers and even judges would be surprised to discover that this legal principle is actually derived from the Bible. It is explained in Hebrews 6 which says, *"For when God made promise to Abraham, because he could swear by no greater, he sware by himself, Saying, Surely blessing I will bless thee, and multiplying I will multiply thee."* Even in secular contracts such as with the business world, a contract has legitimacy only to the degree that it is recognized by some higher power than the two parties entering into the contract which is willing to lend its authority to its legitimacy. In our society, that higher power is usually the state government of the state in which the contract is made or, in some instances, the national government. In either of those instances, it is the civil government which gives legitimacy to a contract and which is the "higher power" who is called upon to enforce the contract in the event of a breach of it by either party. Those "higher powers," then, have the right to exercise authority over the limits of the contract since the higher power is the sovereign which possesses the authority and which is accepting the responsibility to enforce the contract. Therefore the higher power can (and often does) limit the terms of contracts. For the most part, parties (whether individuals or businesses) may bind themselves to whatever terms of a private contract that they wish; but this is not totally without limits. For examples, every state establishes certain basic principles to which all contracts in that state must adhere in order to be legitimate. This is intended to protect both the rights of the parties to the contract, the good order of society in general, and to maintain the integrity of the state, itself. To illustrate this point, no state will recognize a contract which involves any party to the contract committing a crime. Likewise, no state will recognize a contract which does not maintain certain minimum standards that comport with the laws of that state. This is also the reason that each state retains the right (in theory, at least) to establish its own minimum standards with regards to the limits of marriage, including age requirements, restrictions prohibiting close family members from marrying, and (in the past) prohibitions against same sex "marriages." Why the long dissertation on the legal aspects of the terms of contracts, you ask? To get to this point about marriage vows... because marriage is an institution ordained (created) by God, He is the sovereign Who possesses the authority to proscribe the limits of the terms of the marriage contract (covenant). In simple terms, individuals are free to write whatever marriage vows they wish to write and to bind themselves to whatever promises they may wish to make to each other; but they do not possess the authority to set aside the terms of marriage that God has already proscribed in His written Word. At least in a spiritual sense, husbands and wives are bound by the terms of the marriage contract that God has already established; and while they are free to add whatever other beautiful words to those terms that they wish, in His eyes as the Sovereign, no one may create a marriage contract which contravenes any of what He has already established as the marriage covenant. Also, because He is the sovereign who created the institution of marriage, all marriages are subject to His authority – and to the vows that He has established for the institution, even when those marriages involve the lost who refuse to acknowledge His sovereignty. To the lost world, this may seem like just so much jibberish; but for the child of God who understands that "we must all appear before the judgment seat of Christ," it should be what matters the most... that is, what God says are the terms of the marriage covenant and, therefore, what God says are the legitimate reasons for abolishing a marriage through the act of divorce.

Marriage Licenses

Before we continue, I feel compelled to add a brief word about the sanction of marriage by the civil government, primarily owing to the political war fought in recent years by unbelievers to have homosexual unions recognized as legal marriages. I should remind us all that the Bible is to be the rule of faith and practice for every area of our lives; and even when human civil government contradicts the Word of God, it is still the Bible which should be the rule of law for the believer. Daniel and his Hebrew companions in the Old Testament sure believed this. Marriage is an inherently religious exercise; and, therefore, does not fall Scripturally within the sphere of authority of the civil magistrate. It falls more aptly within the sphere of authority of the church in the New Testament, just as it did within the religious system of Israel in the Old Testament. As a theocracy, even the judges in ancient Israel were part of the religious system and were obligated to uphold the laws given by God. Furthermore, because marriage is an institution which was established by God for mankind, He alone as the Sovereign has the authority to proscribe the limitations and the obligations of marriage... which He has done in the written Word of God. To this end, then, any statute which the state may make regarding the institution of marriage which violates the Biblical model of marriage is, in God's eyes, null and void, as the state lacks the proper authority to oversee an institution which it did not create. This truth, of course, is lost on the unsaved mind and, unfortunately, on many believers as well; it is, nevertheless the truth. What is the significance of recognizing this truth? First, it means that even if the state gives its blessings on a union that is outside the one described by God, it is still not a marriage as far as God is concerned and should not be recognized as one by believers, either, no matter the consequences from the world. It is a matter of conscience for which we must all give account one day before the real Judge of this world. Secondly, it also means that believers should give grave consideration to the matter before deciding to accept a marriage "license" from the state. The very word "license" means "permission;" and, from a Biblical worldview, the state (i.e., the civil government) has no genuine authority to grant nor to deny permission to do something when God has already given the permission to do so, provided that the limits set forth by God are observed. Christians have yielded to the civil government in our day far more authority than they are given by God; and when a husband and wife voluntarily accept a marriage license from the state, they have (perhaps inadvertently) made the state a party to the contract when the state previously had no standing to be a party. It is the marriage "license" which makes the state a party to the contract and affords the state far more power over both marriage and divorce than they are intended by God to have. So... believers should consider wisely whether they will even request or sign a marriage "license" before the big wedding day. After all, it is not the license from the state that makes a husband and wife one; it is the covenant that they make with each other and God to become one. Everyone else is merely there to watch and celebrate the occasion with the new bride and groom.

The Act of Marriage

As already stated, it is the taking of vows by the husband and wife which creates the marriage covenant. This contract, in God's eyes, exists the moment that both husband and wife take their vows and enter into the obligation. The physical act which follows, usually on the wedding night, is the consummation of the contract; it is the enjoyment of both husband and wife of the rights that they have obtained as a result of the marriage covenant. No matter what physical pleasures in which the couple may have engaged prior to marriage, those pleasures did not become legal in the sight of God until the marriage vows were made. This consummation of marriage is, therefore, sometimes referred to as "the act of marriage." It is the exercise of the rights one obtains as a result of the marriage covenant. Understanding this is key to understanding why one should not join himself or herself to anyone in this kind of intimate physical relationship until the marriage union is executed through the making of vows together. This is precisely the point that Paul was making in I Corinthians 6:16, *"know ye not that he which is joined to an harlot is one body? for two, saith he, shall be one flesh."* This physical act, though, is much more than just the enjoyment of a husband's rights with his wife as it has historically been viewed. It serves as an outward demonstration in the flesh that the promise is sincere and has been made internally. Such outward acts in the flesh as a sign that one has made sincere vows is not uncommon in the Bible. A few other examples include circumcision in the flesh for the Israelites under the Old Covenant (the Old Testament), baptism for Christians under the New Covenant (the New Testament), the near kinsman taking off his shoe and handing it to Boaz in the beautiful love story of Boaz redeeming Ruth, and God passing between the bodies of the animal sacrifices as a show of His covenant with Abraham.

The physical act of marriage is a demonstration by both husband and wife that they have, in fact, entered into the covenant which they vowed to each other.

Roles in Marriage

Despite modern society's efforts to the contrary, God established distinct and different roles for both husband and wife in a marriage. This does not mean that dad can't help with the cooking and washing dishes; and it also doesn't mean that mom can't help with cutting the grass and changing the oil in the car. What it does mean, however, is that both have a unique role to play in the marriage and, later, in the family involving children. The husband's primary role is that of shepherd; that is, he is to lead his wife along their way in the wonderful adventure as God reveals it to him. During the course of that adventure, he is to provide for the material and spiritual needs of his family and offer both protection and guidance, much the same way that the Lord does each of us as believers. The wife's primary role is to walk alongside her husband as his help meet during their journey in serving God. Her role as help meet means that she supports and bolsters her husband's work and vision for the family. In God's perfect will, it is the husband who is to be led by God and the wife who is to be led by her Godly husband. To be sure, this is antithetical to everything that our modern secular society embraces and attempts to foist upon our children. It is, nevertheless, Biblical; and, hence, the marriage covenant and its accompanying vows are predicated upon this understanding. This is important in order to understand the Biblical grounds for divorce, because it is a breach of the marriage covenant in one or more ways which constitutes a legitimate Biblical ground for divorce. Therefore, understanding and accepting the Biblical roles in marriage – whether society agrees or disagrees – is essential in identifying what things are legitimate and what things are not legitimate reasons for ending a marriage in divorce.

Biblical Admonitions to Husbands and Wives

It is interesting to note that in the New Testament, God chose to give different admonitions to husbands and to wives. This does not mean that the admonitions that we read are the only responsibilities in marriage for the two roles, but most things in marriage concerning the one or the other spouse do seem to neatly fall within these admonitions.

To husbands, the Lord gave the following admonition in Ephesians 5:25, *"Husbands, love your wives, even as Christ also loved the church, and gave himself for it."* And, again, in verse 28, *"So ought men to love their wives as their own bodies. He that loveth his wife loveth himself."* We see clearly here that the primary admonition that the Lord gives to a husband is to love his wife. He even provides two examples of how a husband should love his wife: as Christ loves the church and as a man loves his own body. The picture of Christ's love for the church presents a selfless love and a benevolent love for someone under another's authority. The analogy of a man's love for his own body expresses the truth that we all have a natural inclination to not intentionally hurt our bodies; and that if there is a hurt, we tend to it instead of just letting it hurt. Does the fact that the Lord specifically admonishes husbands to love their wives mean that he is not to also protect, provide, and perform whatever other responsibilities that he may have in marriage? Of course not. As one preacher put it when I was growing up, "Husbands are told to love their wives because this is the single greatest thing that most husbands need to work on." I think that preacher was right. A man who loves his wife in the manner described in Ephesians 5 is probably going to have no problem also wanting to fulfill those other responsibilities to his wife, for they emanate from his selfless love for her. Likewise, I believe that you will see before you finish this book that all of the Biblical grounds for a woman to divorce her husband stem from her husband simply not loving her in the way that God commands.

The same can be said for God's admonition in the New Testament for wives. Just as God's admonition to husbands deals with the thing that husbands must work on the most, so, too, does His admonition to wives deal with the thing which wives must work on the most... because it doesn't come naturally, it must be a choice. Again in Ephesians 5, beginning in verse 22, we read the following: *"Wives, submit yourselves unto your own husbands, as unto the Lord. For the husband is the head of the wife, even as Christ is the head of the church: and he is the saviour of the body. Therefore as the church is subject unto Christ, so let the wives be to their own husbands in every thing."* The word "submit" means exactly what you think that it means. God's command to wives is that they voluntarily place themselves under the authority and oversight of their own husbands. (Note that it does not command them to submit to all husbands, only their *own* husband.) This passage plainly tells us that wives are to submit (that is, to obey) their husbands just as the church is to submit (that is, to obey) Christ. Despite the rising tide of modern feminism, even in the church, this admonition to wives could not be clearer. But just in case there was any confusion in what He intended, the Lord added the following in verse 33, *"Nevertheless let every one of you in particular so love his wife even as himself; and the wife see that she reverence her husband."* The word "reverence" also means exactly what you would think that it means. It means "to honour, respect, show deference to, acknowledge submission to." Again in I Peter 3, the Bible says to wives, *"Likewise, ye wives, be in subjection to your own husbands... Even as Sara obeyed Abraham, calling him lord."* Now the word "lord" here does not mean that she worshipped Abraham as God. The word "lord" here means "master," just as a vassal would acknowledge the lord of the manor as the authority over him and willingly submit to his authority. So, then, it would seem that the number one thing that most wives need to work on is being submissive to their husbands, just as husbands need to work on loving their wives selflessly.

God's Order in the Home

Why did God choose for the husband to be the head of the wife, instead of the other way around? Some might think that He arbitrarily just decided it would be so; and, because He is God, He would have had the authority to just declare it to be that way if He so willed. After all, the Bible tells us in Romans 9, *"Shall the thing formed say to him that formed it, Why hast thou made me thus? Hath not the potter power over the clay, of the same lump to make one vessel unto honour, and another unto dishonour?"* So, then, God has the right to make the husband the head if He wished solely because it was His prerogative; but... that is not the case. I Timothy 2:11 tells us the reason that God chose for women to be in submission, not only in the home but also in the church. He says, *"Let the woman learn in silence with all subjection. But I suffer not a woman to teach, nor to usurp authority over the man, but to be in silence. For Adam was first formed, then Eve. And Adam was not deceived, but the woman being deceived was in the transgression."* In other words, because Eve was deceived by the serpent, God decided that the man would be the better choice as the head of the home... and in the church. This does not mean that Eve was stupid. It means that there was something about how a woman is created that made her more susceptible to certain forms of deception.

This is another of those areas in which modern secular society rages against the teachings of Scripture as being sexist and degrading to women; but nothing could be farther from the truth. It is a simple fact that God made men and women different from each other. Each has specific strengths and weaknesses. For example, when a child falls and scrapes his knee, it is usually to mama or grandma that he goes to have his booboo kissed and made better. Women are intentionally made by God to excel at nurturing. It doesn't mean that men can't or shouldn't; it simply means that, as a general rule, women are better at it. In connection with this difference between women and men, women are, as a general rule, more emotional creatures than men. Again, this is not a defect; it is intentional on God's part in the way that He created male and female because the wife and mom fills a need.

Adam was not deceived in the Garden. He sinned willfully, but he was not deceived. There was something about the makeup of a man that made him less susceptible to the deception that the serpent offered Eve and that she, in turn, offered Adam. As a general rule, men are usually less emotional and rely more upon their reason when making decisions. Sometimes men may take this tendency to a fault by being so unemotional as to be "cold" even in their dealings with loved ones, just as women may sometimes be so overly emotional as to be irrational. Still, though, there was something about the way that God made the man which made him more impervious to deceit and the subtle tricks of the devil. This is why, the Bible tells us, that God placed the man as the head. It also fits right in with the other things contained within the role of a husband as provider and protector. A wise wife is grateful for her husband because he is there to protect her and to provide a covering, a shield of protection for her and the children from dangers without. This is one of the reasons that manhood is under such Satanic attack in our society; for Satan knows that if he can remove the man from the head of any family, the wife and children are easier to attack.

God's choice of the man as the head of the family becomes much easier to accept, especially for wives, when everyone understands the proper way that the husband is supposed to view his wife who has voluntarily submitted to his authority. I Peter 3:7 says, *"Likewise, ye husbands, dwell with them according to knowledge, giving honour unto the wife, as unto the weaker vessel, and as being heirs together of the grace of life; that your prayers be not hindered."* Husbands are to view their wives as "weaker vessels." This in no way means "inferior" or "of lesser value." Quite the opposite is true! It means "weaker" as in "more precious" or "more delicate" – something to be treasured and protected... which is exactly the way that husbands are told repeatedly to love and view their own wives. In our church, I have often used the example of my great aunt's special china that sat in her china cabinet all year long and was only taken out during holiday season when the whole family gathered to eat at Thanksgiving, and Christmas, and, again, on New Year's Day. This was the fine china; it was not meant to be used every day. It was treasured, protected, and viewed as better than the everyday dinnerware. If a husband views his wife in this way, he will treat her the way that God tells husbands to treat their wives. And if wives understand that God views them as special treasures to be nourished and protected by providing a man as their covering, their umbrella of protection, it makes submitting to one's husband a much easier pill to swallow. In a marriage where both the husband and wife acknowledge, respect, and delight in their God-created differences and their God-created roles, there exists the perfect combination of qualities that God intended in a marriage; and husband and wife are both free to enjoy their relationship together while also celebrating the individuality that God has placed within them at the same time.

In the world in which we live today, neither of the two admonitions commanded by God to husbands and wives are popular. In men's circles, husbands are routinely portrayed as weak if they do not "show the wife who's boss" in the household; there are plenty of jokes on the very subject depicted on television daily. By the same token, wives are told that placing themselves under a man's authority is disparaging and degrading to women. This is the sad reality but an accurate depiction of the world's upside down value system and worldview.

When husbands and wives are each in obedience to God, there is no weakness in a man putting his wife before himself; and there is no degradation in a wife submitting to her husband's authority. Biblically, there is a hierarchy which is to be followed in the home, namely this, beginning at the top... God the Father – Christ – husband – wife – children. It's actually very simple to understand; but not always so easy to follow.

Decision-making in Marriage

I must include a word here about decision-making in the home. Knowing what we have just read in Scripture, we already have the Biblical model for decision-making. First of all, anything commanded in the word of God really does not require (or *should* not require) any decision-making on the part of anyone, husband or wife. It should merely be obeyed. In the myriad of other decisions which must be made in a household, though – about everything from the paint on the walls to the house to buy to the church attended to which job to accept – there is a Biblical hierarchy set in place by God to make these decisions.

As we have already seen from Scripture, the husband is the head of the wife; but this does not mean that he has the right or authority to arbitrarily rule as a tyrant over his wife and the children. A husband's legitimacy to his authority emanates from his obedience to God. A husband who is seeking God's will and is obedient to Him, has God's stamp of approval; and that husband's decisions carry the authority of God. This does not mean, however, that a husband should make all of the decisions for the family without seeking the counsel of his wife. Wise is the man who seeks input from his wife, for God gives men and women different vantage points from which to view things; and a wise man will take all of those things into account. Also, a husband who loves his wife selflessly will yield to her desires in any area in which he can do so without detriment to the family. In a marriage in which both husband and wife are sincerely seeking to please God, most decisions can easily be reached by a consensus between the two. In those matters where there is still not agreement, however, even after sincere efforts have been made to reach a consensus, the right of making the final decision for the family must ultimately fall to the husband; for he is the one who must give account to God as the head of the home.

This is not a fact which should be esteemed lightly by either husband or wife; for God will hold him accountable, in this life and the next.

In a home, though, where the wife knows that her husband loves her selflessly, she will have an easier time submitting to his authority, even when she disagrees with his decisions. Likewise, in a home in which the husband sees a sweet and submissive spirit in his wife, he will have an easier time making selfless decisions which will please his wife. It is this synergy between a husband and wife who both love God and are obedient to Him which creates the kind of marriage that God intended for mankind.

Again, in I Peter 3, this is the process being described at work when the Bible says, *"Likewise, ye wives, be in subjection to your own husbands; that, if any obey not the word, they also may without the word be won by the conversation of the wives; While they behold your chaste conversation coupled with fear."* This passage commands wives whose husbands are not seeking to follow God's will to still obey their husbands with respect in the hope that the wife's submissive spirit to her husband will bring conviction upon the husband of his own need to be submissive to Christ. This does not mean that a wife should disobey a Biblical command, however, even if her husband should demand it; but that issue will be dealt with later in this book. A submissive wife's sweet spirit, of course, will have less effect upon an unsaved husband; but then we already have a Biblical command for Christians not to marry unbelievers in the first place. There are occasions, though, when a spouse may become a believer after having already been married to an unbeliever; and there are also occasions in which two Christians actively seeking God's will marry and then one backslides and ceases his or her desire to follow God. In these instances, wives who are still submissive to their husbands with a sweet spirit may bring about sufficient conviction to turn their husbands to Christ; and husbands who love their wives selflessly, even when their wives are not submissive, may yet bring about the necessary conviction to turn the hearts of their wives to Christ.

Conclusion on Marriage

When marriage exists the way that God intends, it is a beautiful picture of Christ and the church – Christ as the bridegroom and the church as His bride. The bridegroom loves His wife selflessly and gave Himself for it. He nourishes, cherishes, protects, and provides for her. The bride of Christ – the church – acknowledges His lordship, submits to His will, and follows Him, her life subsumed into His own as they are one.

All of the Biblical grounds for divorce which are allowed in the Word of God are predicated upon one or more breaches of the marriage covenant; and those breaches always exist because one (or both) of the parties to the covenant did not put into practice the simple truths outlined above.

Part 3

Divorce

I have often heard it said, sometimes even by preachers, that God is never in favour of divorce. This is not true and is, actually, a twisting or perversion of what the Scriptures teach, both about God's rules for man's dealings with each other and also about God's character, itself. A more accurate statement would be that God is never in favour of *the need for* divorce.

Matthew 19:3-18 gives us this dialogue between Jesus and the Pharisees, *"The Pharisees also came unto him, tempting him, and saying unto him, Is it lawful for a man to put away his wife for every cause? And he answered and said unto them, Have ye not read, that he which made them at the beginning made them male and female, And said, For this cause shall a man leave father and mother, and shall cleave to his wife: and they twain shall be one flesh? Wherefore they are no more twain, but one flesh. What therefore God hath joined together, let not man put asunder. They say unto him, Why did Moses then command to give a writing of divorcement, and to put her away? He saith unto them, Moses because of the hardness of your hearts suffered you to put away your wives: but from the beginning it was not so."* Jesus could not have been plainer in His response: God intends marriage to be for life, and it was only because of the sinfulness of man that He had to make a provision for divorce. Why would man's sinfulness necessitate God taking such a drastic step as approving divorce? It is tied to His very nature... if He did not make provision for divorce in certain situations, He would be condoning the abuse of both the institution of marriage and the innocent party in the marriage. God's attributes of justice and love forbid Him from not allowing divorce in certain situations – that is, those situations which He personally would delineate. Again, as the sovereign who ordained and set in place the institution of marriage, He alone has the authority to specify for what reasons a divorcement may be lawfully granted.

It is clear from everything which we have already seen from Scripture about marriage that God's intention for the institution of marriage is that it would be for life once entered into by a man and a woman. There are certain, limited situations in which God not only allows but even *commands* divorce to take place. We will see in this part of the book what those situations are in which divorce is allowed and those in which it is commanded.

In order to illustrate this point, God included within the pages of Scripture His own divorcement. Jeremiah 3:8 reads, *"And I saw, when for all the causes whereby backsliding Israel committed adultery I had put her away, and given her a bill of divorce; yet her treacherous sister Judah feared not, but went and played the harlot also."* The phrase "bill of divorce" means exactly what you think that it means... a "document of cutting off." God is speaking of His divorcement from Israel, the northern kingdom comprised of ten of the twelve tribes which seceded from the kingdom following the death of Solomon. These ten northern tribes were in rebellion against God from the beginning, even going as far as to set up golden calves to be worshipped in Dan and Bethel so that their people would no longer travel to Jerusalem in the southern kingdom to do their worshipping. As He is with us, God was longsuffering toward Israel and sent her many prophets in an attempt to bring conviction upon her and cause her to return to Him; yet she would not. Finally, in 721 B.C., this northern kingdom of Israel was taken into captivity by Assyria who then scattered the people to the four corners of their empire so that they could not mount a revolt at a later date. These are the Israelites oftentimes referred to in some circles as "the ten lost tribes of Israel" because, unlike the southern kingdom of Judah who was allowed to return to the land after her own captivity in Babylon, God did not allow them the same opportunity. So, then, God not only *allows* divorcement in certain circumstances; sometimes He *requires* it.

The Necessity of Divorce

It may seem harsh – and to some, perhaps even blasphemous – to claim that there is value in the right of divorce; yet there are several reasons that there is value in the right of divorce beyond its overt allowances and commandments in Scripture. In fact, the right of divorce is absolutely necessary for these reasons.

The first of these reasons is that divorce (when it occurs with Biblical grounds) upholds an accurate image of God. As the sovereign who created the institution of marriage – and the authority who upholds it – His character and very nature are maligned and slandered if a "marriage" is allowed to exist which does not equate with the institution which He created. God is a covenant-keeping God. We already established that when we discussed the very meaning and importance of His name revealed to His people. When a marriage is allowed to continue to exist in the absence of covenant-keeping, it creates an inaccurate picture of Who our God is. Likewise, a marriage which has been breached and is allowed to continue in that state creates a very unBiblical and inaccurate picture of the relationship between Christ and the church. Again, as previously discussed, the marriage relationship is intended to portray Christ's relationship with His church, both to the lost and to the saved, as a testimony. A marriage which does not accurately portray that relationship is, in legal terms, a "sham," something which is not what it is purported to be.

A second reason that divorce under these circumstances has value is that it is often the act of divorce which alone is harsh enough to move the offending party in the marriage to repentance and to change. This important fact can not be overlooked, for it is always God's desire for anyone who is in sin to be brought to repentance in order that they might be reconciled unto Himself, whether it be the lost in need of salvation or the saved in need of restoring broken fellowship. As I once heard my pastor say when I was growing up, "Forgiveness is the greatest need that anyone has." He went on to explain that that includes forgiveness from those we have wronged here as well as, more importantly, from God, Himself. Many times, the guilty party who has broken the marriage covenant will not see the need to repent as long as the "sham" is allowed to continue. In this instance, the offended party may try in vain to bring about repentance; but as long as the sham is allowed to exist, the guilty may see no reason to repent.

Yet another reason is that divorce allows healing to commence for the wronged party. This may include all aspects of healing including mentally, emotionally, and spiritually. Continuing to exist in a broken marriage, particularly when certain types of abuse are present, prevents the innocent party from healing. In addition to the physical absence of the offender, the wronged party is able to find peace and begin the process of healing.

And finally, it allows the faithful party in the marriage to have the opportunity to find a relationship that is what God intended marriage to be. As long as the offender and offended are bound in a marriage relationship, the offended is prevented, both in a practical sense and in a legal sense, from moving on and pursuing the right kind of relationship with someone else who also wishes to have a Biblical marriage. Divorce frees the innocent party to their marital obligations in the eyes of others even if they were free in God's eyes previously.

The Breaking of the Marriage Covenant

The marriage covenant is broken when there is a breaking of the marital vows – that is, the vows that God has established as the rules for marriage. By entering into the institution which He created, a husband and wife have necessarily submitted themselves to His authority and His rules, even if they should say otherwise. The marriage vows are the binding promises which create the marriage covenant; and these promises create obligations on the part of both parties. This is important because each of the Biblical grounds for divorce is tied to the breaking of one or more of the vows that are implicit in the marriage covenant.

Because the marriage covenant is a binding contract, both legally and spiritually, it is the breaking of the marriage vows which constitutes a breach of contract. A "breach of contract" occurs any time that one of the parties to the contract fails to perform one or more of their promised obligations under the terms of the contract. Similarly, Black's Law Dictionary defines a breach of contract as "a legal cause of action in which a binding agreement is not honored by one or more of the parties to the contract by non-performance or interference with the other party's performance." So then, in simple terms, the breaking of the vows breaches the marriage contract.

In general terms, what is the consequence for breaching a contract? When a breached contract results in one of the parties not receiving the obligations that were promised, the offended party may void the contract. When the contract is voided, the offended party is freed from performing any further obligations under the contract and may also be entitled to damages suffered from the loss of promises under the contract. A discussion of potential damages related to divorce is beyond the intended scope of this book; but what is most important, however, is the fact that the breach may lead to the contract being voided and ending the contractual relationship. In other words, the innocent party is not obligated to stay in the marriage and is free to leave in full possession of the right to remarry and enter into a marriage covenant with someone different.

It is important to understand, however, that a marriage covenant cannot and should not be terminated for just any reason, even if that reason is true. Divorce should not be taken lightly and is intended by God to be permanent. Prior to the War for American Independence, our Founding Fathers sent the Declaration of Independence to King George III outlining the breaches of contract on the part of England toward the colonies. Thomas Jefferson, who wrote the Declaration, included this statement in the document: "Prudence, indeed will dictate that *Governments long established should not be changed for light and transient causes*; and accordingly all experience hath shewn, that mankind are more disposed to suffer, while evils are sufferable, than to right themselves by abolishing the forms to which they are accustomed." The word "light" means "minor" and the word "transient" means "temporary." In other words, he was saying that we as Americans recognize that serious covenants – such as the one between the mother country and her colonies – should not be ended because of a minor infraction or because of a temporary lapse in fulfillment of the obligations by the mother country. Such is also the case in a marriage covenant; no marriage should be abrogated for minor reasons, even if real, nor for temporary failure to fulfill one's responsibilities in the marriage.

All breaches of the contract are not equal. There is a difference in someone wishing to divorce because the spouse has, for example, committed adultery and a situation in which the spouse refused to perform their marital obligations in the physical act of marriage one night because of getting angry during a disagreement, however unfortunate the situation might be. The offending spouse is guilty of breaking the marriage covenant in both instances; but one is for "light and transient causes." If, perhaps, the refusal to perform one's marital obligations involving the physical act of marriage becomes permanent – or even longterm – that could move the infraction from the "light and transient" category into a more serious one.

The point is that marriage is sacred and should be neither entered into nor dissolved with only light considerations taken into account. For both conscience sake and for preserving the sanctity of the institution of marriage, divorce should be initiated only when there is a serious breach of the marriage contract. Even in courts established by man, judges are prohibited by law from voiding contracts merely on the grounds of light or transient infractions. What courts use as the measuring stick in such cases is whether the relationship or the benefits of the relationship are substantially different – materially different – than what was promised in the contract. If one party is getting something substantially different from the contractual relationship than what was promised, the courts have the authority to void the entire contract; but minor or temporary violations of the contract are not generally sufficient to void the contract.

For example, two men entered into a partnership to create a business together as equal owners; as equal owners, the contract stated that no promotional or branding materials would be produced for the company without the approval of both men. Then, without seeking a thumbs up from his partner, one of the men authorized the purchase of promotional brochures for an upcoming sale. He spent $5,000 on the materials in violation of the contractual agreement. His partner was incensed, probably because by this point there were a dozen other things that he had learned about his new business partner that irked him daily.

When he asked the court to abrogate the contract, however, the judge ordered the partner who ordered the promotional materials to reimburse the company for the $5,000 but ruled that the act was not of such consequence that it substantially altered the relationship created by the contract. If this sounds like an absurd example, it is eerily similar to numerous instances in which wives, irked by their husbands' bad habits, convince themselves that they are entitled to a divorce when the husband shells out $5,000 for a new boat without her permission... or when husbands do the same thing because their wives who irritate them with their bad habits spend $5,000 on furniture for the house without asking his permission. Neither of these situations, though, rises to the level of necessitating a divorce, at least not in and of themselves. Hopefully you can see how there is a significant difference between minor or temporary infractions versus those which substantially change the relationship that was agreed to by both parties when they took their wedding vows and entered into holy matrimony.

Some breaches of the marriage covenant are immediate while others may be gradual and cumulative over time. Instances of a major breach which may be immediate are adultery and physical abuse. Both of these examples constitute breaches of the contract in a serious form even if they should only occur on one occasion. The announcement from a spouse that they are abandoning the marriage may also constitute such a breach if they, in fact, depart when they make such an announcement. Other breaches of the marriage contract, however, may still be major breaches which rise to the level of divorce though they be gradual and stretched out over a prolonged period of time. Such cumulative breaches may include prolonged mental and emotional abuse, extended periods of denying one's spouse the marital rights pertaining to the physical act of marriage, or a husband depriving his wife of basic material needs including proper food, clothing, medical care, essential products for hygiene, or the like. In these instances, there is certainly a violation, again, of some of the most basic components of the marriage covenant; but the question becomes whether the deficiency is "light and transient" or whether it is repeated, longterm, and genuinely a crisis. There is a point at which such gradual deprivations may rise to the level of a breach of the marriage contract. Others outside the marriage – and sometimes even the victim in the marriage – may be reluctant to acknowledge the gradual breach as serious; but there is still the possibility that this type of mistreatment, too, may rise to the level of an actual breach of the marriage covenant just as much as the acts of adultery or abandonment.

The question may arise, "In how many different ways or on how many occasions must a marriage covenant be broken before there is legally a breach of contract, at least in God's eyes?" The Bible recognizes something known as "The Law of Contracts," just like secular law recognizes it. Galatians 3:15 says, "Brethren, I speak after the manner of men; Though it be but a man's covenant, yet if it be confirmed, no man disannulleth, or addeth thereto." The passage means that once a covenant (a contract) is confirmed, or entered into, by the parties, none of the parties may unilaterally decide to not perform one or more of his or her obligations and, likewise, none of the parties may require any additional obligations from the party which are not part of the original covenant. Again, as we have previously discussed, a husband and wife may create their own vows and lists of obligations to each other when they marry; but all of those must fall within the "rules" proscribed by God in the Bible in order for them to be binding. Once the marriage covenant is created, however, all parties to the contract are obligated to keep every part of the agreement. In this light, then, breaking even one of the vows of the marriage covenant is a breach of contract; and breaking one of the vows even once is a breach of contract. The question of whether the breach is immediate or gradual may still come into play; but the point is that at whatever time the immediate or cumulative acts constitute a breaking of any of the vows, the offended party has Biblical grounds for divorce.

Part 4

What are the Biblical Grounds?

An Introduction to this Chapter

First, we must not begin this section of the book without understanding that it is vitally essential that divorce not even be a consideration by husbands and wives if there has been no breach of the marriage covenant. One or both spouses may be angry, upset, disappointed, or unhappy with each other; but unless the other party has actually broken the covenant through one of the ways outlined in Scripture as demonstrated in the remainder of this section of the book, there are no Biblical grounds for a divorce. I can not state this too clearly. Before we enter upon a discussion of what the Biblical grounds for divorce are that are contained within the pages of Scripture, everyone (including the reader) is obligated to acknowledge that if none of the following Biblical grounds for divorce exist, divorce should not be under consideration; there are alternatives to help restore the relationship to a healthy marriage before things rise to the need for divorce, and these alternatives are worth exploring, both for the sake of the marriage... and your own conscience before God.

Are Old Testament Biblical Grounds Still In Effect Today?

Secondly, we must address the age-old question that arises when dealing with the subject of divorce from the Word of God, namely: "Didn't Jesus do away with any Biblical grounds for divorce in the Old Testament during His earthly ministry in the New Testament?" Most who answer this question in the affirmative rely primarily upon a passage of Scripture found in Matthew 19:9 and also recorded in Luke in which Jesus is quoted as saying, *"And I say unto you, Whosoever shall put away his wife, except it be for fornication, and shall marry another, committeth adultery: and whoso marrieth her which is put away doth commit adultery."* If this verse is taken either out of context – or without an understanding of the context – it could definitely appear that Jesus is completely abolishing all of the Biblical grounds for divorce given in the Old Testament except adultery. We know that this is not true, however, first of all, because the Apostle Paul later in the New Testament gives yet another Biblical ground for divorce – abandonment by an unbelieving spouse – in I Corinthians 7:15 which states, *"But if the unbelieving depart, let him depart. A brother or a sister is not under bondage in such cases."* Jesus is not only the Son of God but also God in the flesh; He would not have said in the beginning of the New Testament that there was only one Biblical ground for divorce and then later recanted and admitted a second Biblical ground also under the New Covenant. So what, then, is the explanation?

To understand what Jesus was saying in Matthew 19:9, it is of the utmost importance that we rightly divide the Word of God; that is, that we do what we should always do when reading any passage of Scripture... ask ourselves some basic questions, such as: Who is speaking? To whom is He speaking? Why is He addressing this question? What was the issue being raised? ...and perhaps other questions. In this particular situation, the Pharisees are the ones asking the question; and their reason for asking it is that they are trying to get Him to make a mistake with His answer. Jesus' reason for answering it was to provide a Biblical answer and, at the same time, bring judgment upon those who thought they were wiser than He. The context which would escape the casual reader who happened upon Matthew 19 and did not have the advantage of understanding the issue which is repeatedly addressed in the Old Testament is that the Jews had fallen into the trap of acting like the heathen Canaanites around them (who they were supposed to have destroyed already). Jewish men, both in the Old Testament and on into the era in which Jesus lived, had twisted and abused portions of the Mosaic Law in order to dump their existing wives in favour of some pretty, younger ones. We will see the exact passages in the remainder of this chapter; but the point of those Old Testament passages was that men MUST divorce their wives if they treated them as less than wives or if they treated them as less than any *additional* wives that they might marry. The men of Israel had twisted God's command for them to grant their wives divorces in those situations into meaning that they were free to divorce their wives anytime that they wished if they ceased being pleased with their wives. So, then, what Jesus was addressing was NOT that there are not other Biblical grounds for divorce which exist. Rather, what He was addressing was that the fleshly Jewish men were not *allowed* to divorce their wives unless the wives had committed adultery; in other words, they could not just throw their wives away as they had been doing without it being sin on the part of the husband and whoever then married her since, in God's eyes, nothing had happened to breach the marriage covenant and the two were still married as far as He was concerned.

This sinful practice among the Jewish men was what Jesus was addressing, not the question of whether any other Biblical grounds existed for divorce; but too many Christians, including preachers, misinterpret Jesus' teaching here because they have not read it with the proper context or understanding about what the discussion actually concerns. I have heard (and read) far too many preachers who have ignorantly stated that there is no need to examine any grounds for divorce that were granted by God in the Old Testament because Jesus negated all of them except adultery in this one statement. Nothing could be further from the truth. In fact, Jesus said in Matthew 5:17, *"Think not that I am come to destroy the law, or the prophets: I am not come to destroy, but to fulfil."* Jesus, clearly, was not eliminating the other Biblical grounds for divorce; He merely was not addressing them because they were not the issue that He was addressing to the sinful Pharisees. In fact, if anything, we are held to a higher standard of behaviour as New Testament believers because, as the Book of Hebrews tells us, we have a better covenant, a better High Priest, and better promises. Jesus, Himself, said, *"Ye have heard that it was said by them of old time, Thou shalt not commit adultery:* **28***But I say unto you, That whosoever looketh on a woman to lust after her hath committed adultery with her already in his heart."* (Matthew 5:27,28). If God holds New Testament believers to a higher standard of conduct, then husbands (and wives) certainly must fulfill their marital obligations if they do not wish for their spouse to have a Biblical ground for divorce.

There are also some, even well-meaning preachers in good churches, who erroneously state that because Christians are under the New Covenant, we are no longer under the "law," meaning the Mosaic Law of the Old Testament Israelites. As rational as this may sound, it is not sound doctrine. While it is true that the the Mosaic Law and the Old Covenant are not applicable to New Testament Christians, as Paul reminds us countless times in his epistles, it is not true that the moral laws of the Old Testament are no longer applicable to us. The Mosaic Law is comprised of three divisions of laws: moral laws, religious (or ritual) laws, and civil laws. The religious, or Levitical laws, were intended solely for Israel to make them a holy, distinct people from the heathen nations around them; and those laws are not applicable to Christians today under the New Covenant. The moral laws, however, are a reflection of the very character of God, Himself, and are binding upon every man and woman who has ever lived; these include not only the Ten Commandments but all of the moral laws that God gave Moses for Israel concerning right and wrong... including marriage and divorce. Then, finally, there are the civil laws which God gave Israel for their dealings with their fellow man in order to live together in a polite society; we are not obligated to live by these same laws in our own country today; but, to the degree that we do, our country will have the blessings or cursings of God upon our nation. The significance of this discussion about the Mosaic Law and Christians today is that we are still bound by the moral laws of God, just as all men were bound by them even before there was an Israel or a Moses. This includes God's laws about marriage and divorce and the Biblical grounds for both.

A Final Plea to Read the Previous Chapters

The third point that I must emphatically reiterate before continuing is that you, the reader, absolutely must read the preceding chapters of this book in order to have a full understanding of what is presented in the remainder of this book. If you've just thumbed through the table of contents and skipped right to this section, you are making a grave mistake. You are also likely to take any one of the following Biblical grounds for divorce out of their proper context of marriage and divorce that are discussed from the Bible in the preceding chapters. I hope that you will not make this mistake. I hope that you will read all of the preceding chapters before entering in upon the rest of this present chapter. You will be doing a disservice to yourself, your spouse, God, and probably others if you do not read the previous chapters of this book before continuing on.

Biblical Ground #1: Adultery

Perhaps the best place to begin in listing the Biblical grounds for divorce that are given in Scripture is adultery. It is certainly the most fundamental breach of the marriage covenant. All the way back in the Garden of Eden – which was a real place with a real man and woman, by the way – God created the institution of marriage and laid out a very simple, basic understanding of it. The relationship is to be the union, both physically, mentally, emotionally, and spiritually, of a husband and wife. This union is to be so complete that there is to be no room for anyone to exist between the two. This is what is meant in Genesis 2:24 which states, *"Therefore shall a man leave his father and his mother, and shall cleave unto his wife: and they shall be one flesh."* The word "cleave" means "separated;" and, in this sense, it means separated unto something instead of separated from something. That is, the man is to be separated unto his wife... "and they shall be one flesh." It is impossible to separate one from his own flesh; and so it is intended to be with the marriage bond. Marriage is to be a mutually exclusive intimate relationship that permits no one else.

God's view on this subject is no different under the New Covenant, either, which we see reaffirmed by the very words of Jesus in Matthew 19: *"And he answered and said unto them, Have ye not read, that he which made them at the beginning made them male and female, And said, For this cause shall a man leave father and mother, and shall cleave to his wife: and they twain shall be one flesh? Wherefore they are no more twain, but one flesh. What therefore God hath joined together, let not man put asunder."* Jesus not only quoted the words of His Father as recorded in Genesis but then went on to give His own commentary on the meaning of it when He finished with the words, *"What therefore God hath joined together, let not man put asunder."* His explanation was so concise yet so profound that it is still today included in virtually every wedding ceremony conducted in the Christian world.

And just to make sure that there was no room for doubt about whether God's view on the matter was different after His setting up of the New Testament church, He also had Paul, the apostle to the Gentiles and the one to whom was revealed the mystery of the church, reaffirm the very same view in Ephesians 5: *"So ought men to love their wives as their own bodies. He that loveth his wife loveth himself. For no man ever yet hated his own flesh; but nourisheth and cherisheth it, even as the Lord the church: For we are members of his body, of his flesh, and of his bones. For this cause shall a man leave his father and mother, and shall be joined unto his wife, and they two shall be one flesh. This is a great mystery: but I speak concerning Christ and the church. Nevertheless let every one of you in particular so love his wife even as himself; and the wife see that she reverence her husband."* Paul tells us that God's view of marriage is what it is, in part, because it is His desire for it to portray His relationship with the bride of Christ, the church.

Adultery may be defined as any sexual relationship outside the boundaries of the marriage relationship between a husband and wife. There are other ways in which a husband or wife may allow someone else into the marriage in an unBiblical way, as well; but we will discuss that later. For now, we are concerned solely with adultery. Literally speaking, adultery is committing the physical act of marriage with anyone who is not a party to the marriage covenant. It is the very act, itself – the physical act. This is clearly what is conveyed in John 8 in the story of the woman taken in adultery which states, *"And the scribes and Pharisees brought unto him a woman taken in adultery; and when they had set her in the midst, They say unto him, Master, this woman was taken in adultery, in the very act."* It is the physical act, itself, which constitutes adultery. This is also clearly attested to when the Lord speaks of the spirit of Jezebel in Revelation 2:22 which has permeated many churches right up to today: *"Behold, I will* cast her into a bed, and them that commit adultery with her into great tribulation..." In Proverbs 7, the Bible describes a woman who commits adultery while her husband is away: *"And, behold, there met him a woman with the attire of an harlot, and subtil of heart... So she caught him, and kissed him, and with an impudent face said unto him, I have peace offerings with me; this day have I payed my vows. Therefore came I forth to meet thee, diligently to seek thy face, and I have found thee. I have decked my bed with coverings of tapestry, with carved works, with fine linen of Egypt. I have perfumed my bed with myrrh, aloes, and cinnamon. Come, let us take our fill of love until the morning: let us solace ourselves with loves. For the goodman is not at home, he is gone a long journey: He hath taken a bag of money with him, and will come home at the day appointed."* And, again, in Ezekiel 23:7 we find a description of adultery which presents the actual physical act, *"Thus she committed her whoredoms with them, with all them that were the chosen men of Assyria, and with all on whom she doted: with all their idols she defiled herself. Neither left she her whoredoms brought from Egypt: for in her youth they lay with her."* When the Bible says here that they "lay" with her, it means that they lay in the bed and committed the physical act with her.

Grammatically, even the verb associated with adultery necessarily implies an act as opposed to feelings, thoughts, or emotions. In the giving of the Ten Commandments, Exodus 20:14 tells us, *"Thou shalt not commit adultery."* The very word "commit" involves an act. One "commits" adultery, murder, theft, arson, breach of contract, etc. One does not "commit" lust, envy, grief, or pride. No, the verb "commit" is reserved for an act, not a feeling. This does not mean, of course, that some of those feelings are not wrong; for they clearly are sins. What it means, though, is that to commit adultery, one must commit an act – the physical act reserved for marriage – with someone outside the marriage covenant.

The significance of the physical act of marriage cannot be overstated. It is the physical act which consummates the marriage covenant. It is the physical act which moves the marriage covenant from mere words to action; it is the acting upon of the covenant, itself. And it is precisely the seriousness of this act which, when committed with anyone outside the marriage covenant, constitutes the most basic breach of the marriage covenant; for in committing this act of physical union with another, the marriage partner has necessarily become one with another to whom he or she is not covenanted and has, in so doing, given to someone else what is exclusively reserved for the spouse in the binding promises that were made at the time that marriage vows were exchanged. I Corinthians 6:16 says very clearly, *"know ye not that he which is joined to an harlot is one body? for two, saith he, shall be one flesh."* As a covenant-keeping God, our God takes this matter very seriously and expects mankind to do the same, both in our relationship with Him and also with each other.

As we have already seen, Jesus scolded the Pharisees for approving of men divorcing their wives merely because they were tired of them and wanted to marry someone else. In so doing, though, He also made it clear that the act of adultery *does* constitute Biblical grounds for divorce. In Matthew 5:31 and 32, He says, *"It hath been said, Whosoever shall put away his wife, let him give her a writing of divorcement: But I say unto you, That whosoever shall put away his wife, saving for the cause of fornication, causeth her to commit adultery: and whosoever shall marry her that is divorced committeth adultery."* Jesus here uses the word "fornication" for adultery. The word "fornication" includes any sexual act outside the bounds of marriage and can incorporate everything from adultery to homosexuality to beastiality to even mere sex between two consenting adults prior to marriage. Specifically, "adultery" refers solely to a sexual act committed by a married person with someone who is outside the marriage covenant; therefore, Jesus is correct in identifying "adultery" with any type of fornication committed by a married person. Logically speaking, all forms of fornication constitute adultery for a married person; but adultery is a distinct form of fornication which can only be committed by someone who is either married or by someone who is committing the act with a person who is married to another.

Case Study: Kathy and Albert had been married for sixteen years and even had a couple of children together when Kathy became bored in their marriage and began a flirtatious relationship with a younger man from work. By the time Albert discovered the affair, Kathy had already slept with her co-worker on multiple occasions. By this point, however, Kathy had become disillusioned with the "exciting" new relationship and begged Albert to forgive her adulterous affair. Because Kathy had already committed the physical act of adultery, both she and her co-worker were guilty of adultery according to Scripture. Albert had Biblical grounds to divorce his wife if he chose and was left with a personal decision to make that would affect both him and his children who were all three unwitting victims of the sin.

In the same chapter of Matthew, just a few verses earlier, Jesus also said, *"Ye have heard that it was said by them of old time, Thou shalt not commit adultery: But I say unto you, That whosoever looketh on a woman to lust after her hath committed adultery with her already in his heart."* This is in keeping with what the Scripture says in Proverbs 23:7: *"For as he thinketh in his heart, so is he."* The man (or woman) who dwells upon the thought of adultery is an adulterer; and, given the right time and the right circumstance, he or she will commit the act of adultery. Such is the reason that He also commands us in Proverbs 4:23 to *"Keep thy heart with all diligence; for out of it are the issues of life."* God places a high premium on fidelity, or faithfulness, within the bounds of marriage, as evidenced by this statement. He expects spouses to be faithful to one another.

Perhaps a word of caution is necessary here. While Jesus clearly is teaching that spouses have a higher standard of commitment toward each other than merely not committing the *act* of adultery, I doubt that He would be pleased with anyone abusing His statement, either. For example, a wife who used the excuse that she caught her husband staring at a beautiful woman who walked by as a basis for wanting a divorce would, I think, be in error. Likewise, the husband who threatens to divorce his wife because she made a comment about finding her favourite actor handsome would also be in the same error. Either of these situations could be symptomatic of greater problems in the marriage that may meet other Biblical grounds for divorce; but on their own, I'm quite certain that they would fail to meet God's strict views of allowable divorce.

In order to demonstrate how strong His feelings are on the matter of adultery, God divorced Israel... literally. Jeremiah 3:8 says, "And I saw, when for all the causes whereby backsliding Israel committed adultery I had put her away, and given her a bill of divorce; yet her treacherous sister Judah feared not, but went and played the harlot also." Israel had joined herself to other gods in idolatry, repeatedly and habitually breaking the marriage covenant that she made with Jehovah God at the foot of Mount Sinai in Exodus 19 until finally she had exhausted the grace and mercy that He was willing to allow her... and He divorced her. It only takes one time of committing the act of adultery to constitute adultery; but God, in His grace and mercy had given Israel chances to repent that He did not have to give before divorcing her. When one reads of the abundant grace and mercy of the Lord throughout the pages of Scripture, especially in His dealings with Israel, surely it cannot escape the reader that God not only acknowledges that there are Biblical grounds that exist for divorce – but there are times when it is good and right and necessary. The adultery of Israel is a clear example.

Biblical Ground #2: Physical Abandonment

Even among Christians, churches, and denominations that refuse to acknowledge the Biblical grounds for divorce which are clearly laid out in the Old Testament, there is a second Biblical ground for divorce which is generally allowed in addition to adultery because it is specifically enumerated in the New Testament: this is physical abandonment.

The Apostle Paul clearly outlined this Biblical ground for divorce in I Corinthians 7 beginning in verse 10: *"And unto the married I command, yet not I, but the Lord, Let not the wife depart from her husband: But and if she depart, let her remain unmarried, or be reconciled to her husband: and let not the husband put away his wife. But to the rest speak I, not the Lord: If any brother hath a wife that believeth not, and she be pleased to dwell with him, let him not put her away. And the woman which hath an husband that believeth not, and if he be pleased to dwell with her, let her not leave him. For the unbelieving husband is sanctified by the wife, and the unbelieving wife is sanctified by the husband: else were your children unclean; but now are they holy. But if the unbelieving depart, let him depart. A brother or a sister is not under bondage in such cases: but God hath called us to peace. For what knowest thou, O wife, whether thou shalt save thy husband? or how knowest thou, O man, whether thou shalt save thy wife?"*

There are several very important points in this passage that we must identify in order to make sure that we are rightly dividing the Word of God and not misinterpreting or misapplying it. First of all, the context of the passage is one in which Paul is writing to the first generation of Christians – that is, to many who had literally just been gloriously saved out of paganism and led to Christ by Paul, himself, or some other disciple; consequently, some of them found themselves in the unenviable position of being a Christian but still married to a pagan unbeliever. This passage is NOT giving license for a Christian to violate Biblical principles and marry an unbeliever; rather, it is merely dealing with the cold hard fact that it *was* not and *still is not* an uncommon thing for someone who becomes a believer to find themselves in a marriage with an unbeliever who has still not yet chosen to accept Christ. These were marriages which were created while both husband and wife were unbelievers, before one or the other of the spouses became a Christian. To those who find themselves in this unenviable position, Paul commands them to not depart. In fact, he specifically tells the readers that this command is from the Lord and are not his own thoughts as an apostle. So, then, we see from this passage that someone who becomes a Christian and is still married to an unbeliever does not have Biblical grounds, in and of this fact, to divorce his or her spouse. This should tells us just how strongly God feels about the sanctity of the marriage covenant. Our covenant-keeping God feels so strongly about the obligation to keep one's covenant that He does not automatically release even His own children from a covenant made with an unbeliever.

The second point which the passage brings out is that if a Christian spouse *does* leave in spite of God's command not to do so, it still does not give the Christian a Biblical ground for divorce. Rather, Paul says that the Christian who departs – in divorce – from his or her spouse should remain unmarried. This necessarily implies that, at least in God's sight, there was no Biblical ground for divorce; and, so, the believer is still technically married and may not enter into a marriage covenant with anyone else while the former covenant still exists. God's purpose in not permitting remarriage in this situation is the hope that, in time, the husband and wife will be reconciled together and the marriage (which was never abrogated in God's eyes) will be restored.

The third major point found in this passage is one in which Paul makes it clear that he is speaking of his own opinion and not of command by God. It is significant that we acknowledge that this is a very rare exception in Paul's writing – or anywhere in Scripture – that one of the human authors makes a point to tell us that he is no longer writing under divine command. This does not mean, however, that the human author (in this case Paul) is not still expressing God's will on the subject; it simply means that God did not command him to say what he is about to say. We should remember, however, that *"all scripture is given by inspiration of God;"* and one would suppose that this includes Paul's comments which he gives here – not by divine command but clearly by divine permission. Therefore, we should not write off Paul's following comments simply because he is speaking by divine permission and not by divine command. I feel certain that the Holy Spirit of God would have forbade him rendering an opinion to his readers that would have resulted in sin on either his part for giving it or their part for following it.

This third point outlined in the passage is one in which Paul argues for a Christian who finds himself or herself in a marriage with an unbeliever to remain in the marriage specifically for the purpose of hopefully winning the spouse to Christ through a testimony of godliness. Again, this in no way is a defense of disobedient Christians who seek to use this as an argument to knowingly marry an unsaved person in the hope of converting them to the Lord; this is uniquely spoken to those who have become Christians, themselves, after having already been married. In all honesty, when Paul makes this argument, he is giving commentary on the previous command from God moreso than he is giving some new thought. What he argues flows logically from what God commanded in the previous statement.

The fourth point in the passage, however, is a new statement and not merely an outflow from God's command. Again, Paul is speaking with God's permission but not by command. The point made is that a Christian who finds himself or herself in a marriage with an unbeliever is freed from the marriage covenant *if the unbelieving spouse* chooses to depart. This is a different scenario entirely from the believing spouse choosing to depart without Biblical grounds. The believing spouse is bound by the marriage covenant to remain in the marriage despite being married to an unbeliever because the believer is expected to obey God's laws. The unbelieving spouse, however, while still honour-bound by the same covenant, may not necessarily feel the same sense of obligation because of his or her lost condition, no matter that the obligation exists nevertheless. In this case, if the unbelieving spouse departs, Paul says the believer is no longer bound by the marriage covenant.

The reason that the believer is no longer bound in such cases is that the departing spouse has breached the marriage covenant (contract) simply by departing. In departing, it becomes impossible for the departing spouse to perform his or her obligations under the covenant; and it also becomes impossible for the remaining spouse to perform his or her obligations owing to the departure of the unbeliever. Returning to a legal definition of a "breach of contract," a breach occurs whenever a party to the contract fails to perform his obligations under the contract or makes it impossible for the other party to perform obligations.

While it is certainly possible for a spouse to abandon marital responsibilities while remaining physically present in the marriage, that is not what is being described by the Apostle Paul in this passage. We will deal with those Biblical grounds later, but the Biblical ground for divorce presented here by Paul is physical abandonment – that is, literally, physically leaving the marriage. Of this we can be certain since Paul emphatically says, *"But if the unbelieving depart, let him depart."*

Case Study: After being married for several years, Cindy decided that she still had some "wild oats" to sow because

she had married in her early twenties. After announcing to her husband Roger one evening that she no longer wished to be married, she quickly moved out one day while he was at work. He returned home to discover that she had gone. In spite of his efforts to get her to return, Cindy was determined not to do so and eventually filed for divorce. Since her husband had given her no Biblical grounds for divorce, Cindy was at fault and in sin by leaving and divorcing her husband, even though the state granted her divorce without question. In reality, Roger was the one who had Biblical grounds for divorce had he chosen to exercise it. Nevertheless, he was unbound from his covenant with her and free to remarry according to Scripture.

We must be cautious, however, not to misappropriate something for the physical abandonment of which Paul is speaking if it is not actually physical abandonment. For example, it is possible that a spouse may be physically absent for a period of time, perhaps even an extended period of time, due to military service, work assignment, or even Christian ministry. The mere absence of a spouse for a period of time does not necessarily, in and of itself, constitute the Biblical ground for divorce. In the event that any of these absences is due to a circumstance which existed prior to the marriage, both spouses knew in advance what these prior existing circumstances were and, by implication, assented to them when marriage vows were exchanged without guarantees of these things being altered or abolished. As long as these circumstances were understood by both parties in advance of the marriage covenant, the absent spouse entered into the marriage contract in good faith, not attempting to mislead the other spouse; and the other spouse assented to these conditions by still agreeing to enter into the marriage covenant without a change. If these circumstances arise after the marriage has been consummated, it should only be admitted after the Biblical plan for decision-making within marriage that we have previously discussed has taken place. This necessarily implies that this set of circumstances be temporary and not permanent. Paul addresses this very possibility earlier in the same chapter of I Corinthians 7 beginning in verse 3 when he says, *"Let the husband render unto the wife due benevolence: and likewise also the wife unto the husband. The wife hath not power of her own body, but the husband: and likewise also the husband hath not power of his own body, but the wife. Defraud ye not one the other, except it be with consent for a time, that ye may give yourselves to fasting and prayer; and come together again, that Satan tempt you not for your incontinency."* Paul is speaking specifically about husbands and wives abstaining from the physical act of marriage, and he precisely admits the possibility that it may be necessary from time to time but only in agreement between the two and only for a time – in other words, it must only be temporary. In fairness to both parties, if one of these extenuating circumstances exists, there must be a specified time that it is expected to last before the two are reunited, including the physical act of marriage. There should never be an open-ended deadline for these circumstances to be brought to a conclusion; there must be hope for both partners that it is coming to an end at a given moment in time or a given event in time... light at the end of the tunnel. The point here is that the mere physical absence of a spouse for one of these legitimate reasons does not necessarily constitute Biblical ground for divorce in and of itself. If a spouse departs physically for the point of abridging the marriage covenant, though – and it becomes more than a transient departure – then the very act of physical abandonment does constitute Biblical grounds for divorce.

Case Study: Jen is married to Jim who is unexpectedly deployed oversees with his national guard unit due to an impending emergency. Although Jen may not have foreseen this as a possibility when they married, Jim is, nevertheless, required to deploy whether he wishes to do so or not. As the

days turn into weeks and then into months, Jen grows increasingly impatient and considers a divorce because Jim is not home to meet her marital needs. Jim's absence, though, even if it becomes an extended one, does not constitute Biblical grounds for divorce as "physical abandonment." There is, as the Apostle Paul says in I Corinthians 7, the very real danger that one or the other of the spouses may yield to sin and temptation during the absence, however, if they do not both remain vigilant and, thereby, create legitimate Biblical grounds for divorce.

The question then inevitably arises, "What if my spouse who departs claims to be a Christian? Am I still bound to remain married after a Christian spouse departs?" The simple answer to this question is that no one is bound to the marriage covenant any longer if the spouse departs, whether the spouse is saved or lost. Paul's comments presuppose that Christians are going to be obedient and follow the Lord's command *not* to depart in the first place. If, however, a spouse who claims to be a Christian physically abandons the marriage, the remaining spouse, whether saved or lost, is still no longer bound to the marriage covenant. Firstly, the act of physical abandonment, as we have just seen, is a breach of the marriage contract which abrogates (or dissolves) the covenant. Secondly, a spouse who purports to be a Christian but acts in the manner of an unbeliever must be viewed as an unbeliever. Only God knows the heart; and since we do not posses the ability to know the heart as God can, we must make our assumptions upon what we do know; and, in this case, a spouse who willfully disobeys God's command and departs must be viewed as an unbeliever until there is some reason to assume otherwise. Our God is not a cruel God. To hold a spouse bound to a marriage covenant which has been abandoned by the other spouse would be cruel, indeed. Our covenant-keeping God is neither cruel nor unlawful in His dealings with His children.

Biblical Ground #3: Leaving and Cleaving

All the way back in the Garden of Eden when the first marriage took place between Adam and Eve, God gave some very basic instructions that included the words, *"Therefore shall a man leave his father and his mother, and shall cleave unto his wife: and they shall be one flesh"* (Genesis 2:24). For more than six thousand years now, these words have been handed down from one generation to the next and still today comprise part of the wedding vows for many couples getting married. This inherent part of the marriage covenant is, again, a component of the compact which was ordained by God. That is, He divinely decreed that it would be so in marriage. Even for couples who do not choose to include these particular words in their own wedding vows, it is still an implicit part of the marriage covenant because it was established as part of the institution by the Creator of the institution. As the Creator of the institution of marriage, God has full sovereignty to determine what the rules will be pertaining to it.

This same part of the marriage covenant is echoed in the New Testament when Jesus says in Mark 10:7 and 8, *"For this cause shall a man leave his father and mother, and cleave to his wife; And they twain shall be one flesh: so then they are no more twain, but one flesh."* And again in Ephesians 5:31 when Paul quotes the Book of Genesis: *"For this cause shall a man leave his father and mother, and shall be joined unto his wife, and they two shall be one flesh."* This very fundamental aspect of the marriage covenant is delivered by God in the very beginning and then repeatedly reaffirmed throughout both the Old and New Testaments.

The word "cleave" means "to separate." Remember, marriage between a husband and wife is intended by God to picture the relationship between Christ and the church; and, just as with that relationship, the Bible tells us that there is something to separate *from* and something to separate *unto*. As Christians – and part of the bride of Christ, the church – we are called to separate *from* sin and *unto* Christ. Similarly, in marriage, a husband is commanded to separate from his father and mother and separate unto his wife. Implicit in this command is that the wife shall do likewise unto her husband.

The word "cleave" is used in numerous passages in Scripture, sometimes referring to a separation from something and sometimes referring to a separation unto something. Another example of cleaving in the Bible which involves separating *from* something is found in Zechariah 14:4 which speaks of the Mount of Olives cleaving in two when Jesus descends from heaven at the Second Coming and literally, physically sets foot again in the same place where He ascended in Acts chapter one. *"And his feet shall stand in that day upon the mount of Olives, which is before Jerusalem on the east, and the mount of Olives shall cleave in the midst thereof toward the east and toward the west, and there shall be a very great valley."* The mountain will literally separate apart from itself in that moment. Another example of something cleaving *unto* something in the Bible is found in Ezekiel 3:26 which says, *"And I will make thy tongue cleave to the roof of thy mouth, that thou shalt be dumb."* In this instance, God says that He would make the tongue separate unto the roof of the mouth so that speaking would be impossible.

When Genesis 2:24 says, *"Therefore shall a man leave his father and his mother, and shall cleave unto his wife: and they shall be one flesh,"* it requires us to look back at the preceding verses to have the proper context concerning the word "therefore" which means "because of what was just said." What was just said in the previous verses? The story of God creating the woman from the rib of the man and bringing her to him to be his mate, of course. So, then, because of this... husbands should leave their fathers and mothers and cleave to their wives. This is God's way of telling us that when a husband and wife come together in the marriage covenant, they are creating a new bond in each of their lives – in essence, they are leaving their previous families for the purpose of creating their own family. This certainly does not mean that they should have no more ties to either of their previous families; but it necessarily means that their new family together, as husband and wife, is, with God at the center, to be their central focus in life. This is why the final part of Genesis 2:24 ends with, "and they shall be one flesh." Because of this new relationship as husband and wife, they are now become as one.

The passage here in Genesis specifically refers to the husband leaving his father and mother; but this is not intended to imply that the wife is not expected to do the same. In every single story of Scripture where we read of husbands and wives, we always see that the wife does the very same thing, as well. In fact, it was just inherently understood in the culture of the time in which the Bible was originally penned that a woman naturally left home to take up residence with her husband in their home together when they were married. There are numerous examples in the Bible of women leaving their homes with parents upon marriage to do this very thing. Wives are expected to follow their husbands as their husbands follow God. This is what is expected by God of both husbands and wives.

It is important that we understand precisely what God is communicating to us in this leaving and cleaving that He mentions in relation to marriage in both the Old and New Testaments. In fact, it is essential, for it is the very fundamental basis for the creation of a marriage and the new family that it brings about. God is literally saying that husbands and wives are to be separated from everyone else in the world (including their own parents who were previously their closest relationships) unto their new spouses, together creating a new unit of one that is so tightly knit together that no one save God can enter in between. Again, it is vitally important that every husband and wife understand the significance of what God is commanding here... that both are to have no higher allegiance to anyone, other than the Lord, than they have to each other. This is explicitly and implicitly what is being stated in Scripture about the marriage covenant.

Case Study: At a young age, Michael married a girl he had met who happened to live about two hours away. When they married, he and his young wife Heather lived for the first year or two near her parents. Because Michael already had a good paying job that he did not wish to give up when they married, it meant that he had to drive about an hour and a half to and from work every day. Before long, though, the drive got old, especially since he had to be at work early every morning; and Michael's mom began encouraging him to just spend the night in his old room after work several times a week instead of driving all the way back to his new home with his wife. Michael had always been close to his mom because his father was an alcoholic who had abandoned them when he was a small child; and, eventually, he gave in to his mother's urging and began spending the night back at his mom's once or twice a week. His young wife tried hard to understand even though it didn't seem right to her; but since she had her own parents nearby, it was bearable. When Michael began staying at his mom's house on Friday nights after work instead of returning home for the weekend, though, it raised even more red flags for Heather.

After just a year or two of being married, Michael's mother purchased two houses side-by-side with one another and invited him and Heather to move into one of the two houses and live rent-free. Since the young couple was already struggling financially, in part because of Michael's tendency

toward impulse buying, they packed up and moved from living near Heather's parents to living right next door to Michael's mom and her live-in boyfriend.

This continued for a number of years, and Michael and Heather had several children of their own along the way. It did not take long, however, for Heather to learn that Michael's mom was the one who "wore the pants in the family," even in Heather's home with Michael. Whether it was because he felt financially tied to her or just because he could not stand up to her because he lacked the spine to do so, Michael always gave in to his mother's demands… and expected his wife to do the same. Anytime that it came down to a disagreement between Heather and his mother, Michael regularly sided with his mother; and anytime that his wife wanted to do something that interfered with his mother's plans, Michael routinely vetoed his wife's plans. Heather's mother-in-law spent plenty of money on them and the kids, but it was the fact that she also wanted to run their lives that bothered Heather. Michael's mother went on vacations with them and, of course, paid for much of them. His mother was not shy, either, about criticizing Heather, even in front of the children. Over the years, Michael's pattern of deferring to his mother's wishes over his wife's ate at Heather; but she was two hours away from her own family and felt isolated with no support nearby, certainly not from her husband. Nevertheless, she tried to be a submissive wife and a good mom, even on the occasions when she confronted Michael about the problems that, by now, had become commonplace in their marriage owing to him allowing his mother to insert herself so intimately into their daily lives. Heather even threatened to leave the marriage if things did not change; and, in spite of Michael's many promises, things remained much the same and always returned to the "normal" after a few days.

Finally the day came when Michael's mother, now older and not in as good of health, announced that she had decided to sell both of the adjoining properties. She had a "sit-down" with Michael and Heather and suggested that the couple buy a house with a "mother-in-law suite," and she would help with the purchase of the home; she and her live-in boyfriend would then move in until they were too old to remain at home. Heather was extremely reluctant to have her mother-in-law even closer than she had been when it was just next door; but Michael saw this as his opportunity to "keep up with the Joneses" and buy the large house of his dreams. Because of his impulse buying over the years, the couple's credit was a mess; and he and Heather would never have been able to purchase a nice home together, even with both of their incomes. This was the chance of a lifetime... at least for him.

Michael and Heather moved into a spacious home, along with their children, his mother, and her still-live-in boyfriend. It wasn't long, however, before it became apparent to Heather that this was the mistake that she had been afraid it would be. That first Christmas in the new home found Heather excited about decorating her new home for the holidays; and she was more than a little upset when Michael allowed his mother to have veto power over which decorations would be used inside and outside the house, even substituting some of her own decorations, which Heather found gaudy, to replace some of the ones that his wife had purchased. The decorations, however, were only a hint of things to come. Michael's mother soon became the matriarch of the home, deciding everything from what would be served for meals (even though she, herself, did little of the cooking) to deciding on what the couple "could" spend their own money. She increasingly interloped in the raising of the children, at first settling for "correcting" Michael and

Heather in front of the children whenever she disagreed with their rules or disciplinary methods. Whenever Michael and Heather were at work and the children were home from school, she routinely allowed the children to defy the rules of their parents and even went so far as to allow the children to miss school without their parents' permission since Michael and Heather were both at work early each day. Even worse, it became more and more obvious that Michael's mother did not share the same Christian convictions that Heather had instilled in her own life since she was a teenager, herself; and now, living under the same roof, her mother-in-law's worldly lifestyle increasingly showed itself, even in front of the children.

Over time, Michael's disregard for Heather's wishes over his mother soon spread to the children who learned from their father that it was "okay" to disregard their mother's rules and directions as long as they could get their grandmother to side with them... which she invariably did, simply to usurp Heather's role in the household if for no other reason.

At some point, Heather reached her breaking point and threatened to leave. After much crying and pleading – and bringing the children into his and Heather's bedroom so that he could show the children that their mother was contemplating leaving – Michael compelled Heather to stay by promising to go to marriage counseling with their pastor. After all, how could she leave with her children brought into the room and terrorized by Michael crying and telling them to plead with her right in front of her very eyes?

Michael did, in fact, attend counseling – both jointly and individually – with their pastor... for a short time. Their pastor barely knew Michael because, even though Heather and the children had attended church faithfully for several years since joining, he had only occasionally attended, mainly for special services. The counseling that Michael had promised to attend faithfully now in the face of his wife leaving lasted only about as long as it took for the family to settle back into the usual routine and for the immediate danger of Heather leaving to pass. Within less than two months, Michael simply stopped showing up for his counseling sessions; and within weeks of making the myriad of promises to Heather and to the pastor that he had made about fixing his own problems in the marriage that he readily acknowledged on his own, he had ceased following through with all but the easiest ones of them. Only the items which were easily seen by others and created a facade remained. And when the next big issue with his mother interfering in the marriage arose, Michael was not bashful about acknowledging that he had come to the conclusion that "it was just the way that it was going to be as long as his mother was alive." In effect, after all of the counseling regarding the Biblical role of husband and wife and the Biblical mandate to allow no one to separate between spouses in a marriage, Michael had decided that because of the couple's financial dependency upon his mother, he could not (or would not) stand up to her. In Heather's estimation, it was not so much his mother's money that ruled the day as it was the fact that Michael still was too closely tied to his mother's apron strings. Whichever the reason, Michael had clearly allowed someone else to separate between husband and wife in the marriage and had given someone else the proper role that was owed to his wife and the mother of his children. In her own home where she was the wife and mother, Heather was prevented and denied her rightful role.

This is a rather lengthy case study – in part because Heather patiently and submissively stayed as long as she did, hoping that things would change, always at the "next" chapter of their marriage... but it never did. And in part, it is a long case study because it was necessary in this book to attempt to illustrate how Michael allowed another person to separate between him and his wife even though the other person was a non-sexual relationship. Though this was not a case of an extramarital affair with someone outside the marriage, it was, nevertheless, a violation of the original marriage covenant that God created in the Garden of Eden and a violation of His command to separate from all others in the creation of the unique marriage relationship where husband and wife become one and there exists no room for anyone between the two. Michael allowed someone else to assume the rights and authorities of his wife; and it was a breach of the marriage covenant. Ultimately, even Michael reluctantly admitted that it was so... and that he had no intention of taking the necessary steps to change it; he chose his mother's approval and his mother's financial cushion over his wife.

The point of the previous case study is not that there was a breach of the marriage covenant because the husband allowed his mother to live in the same house with him and his wife. Rather, it was a matter of him allowing his mother (or anyone) to usurp the rights and authorities that belonged to his wife and the mother of his children. It was his choice of allowing someone – anyone – to come between him and his wife. I feel the need to make this as crystal clear as possible because there is nothing inherently wrong with allowing a parent or anyone else to live in the same dwelling as the husband, wife, and children. In fact, the Bible provides numerous examples of multi-generational families living together without this breach of the marriage covenant. Indeed, for many cultures, even in the modern world, having elderly parents or relatives in the extended family such as nieces, nephews, cousins, or siblings living in the same dwelling with the husband, wife, and children is the norm. Couples who choose to take care of the elderly parents of one or both spouse when it becomes necessary for physical reasons should be praised, not castigated for the decision. There is nothing inherently contravening of the marriage contract in having other people living in the same residence. It is not until someone other than a spouse is given the rights or authorities due only to the two spouses that a breach has occurred; and it is the spouse who gives deference to or respects the usurpation by another who is the party at fault.

This breach may be made by the wife just as well as by the husband; and it may be made by either spouse allowing someone other than just a parent to assume some or all of the spousal rights that belong to the marriage partner. While it is the parents that Scripture specifically singles out as those that a man must leave when cleaving to his wife (and vise versa), the Word of God is not intending to suggest that other parties cannot usurp the place that a spouse is to have inside the marriage covenant, either. As we have seen already, a husband and wife are to have each other's highest loyalty above everyone else save the Lord, Himself. All others, no matter their relation or standing, are to be placed beneath the spouse in terms of allegiance.

Another common example of one spouse unBiblically allowing someone else to have a place of higher allegiance than husband or wife is the situation in which a child or children are given this place. As we saw in the earlier portion of this book dealing with the marriage covenant itself, both spouses are to have a love and dedication to raising the children of the family in the nurture and admonition of the Lord. Unfortunately, it is not unusual for one or both spouses to allow the children in the family to have their allegiance over their spouse. I have seen situations in which this occurred because there were already other problems in the marriage and the children were ascribed an inappropriate place in one spouse's affections as a passive aggressive way to disrespect the other spouse. After all, it's much less likely that anyone is going to correct a parent for showing affection for their own child, even if it is being done in a disloyal manner toward their spouse. I have also seen situations, though, where this inappropriate treatment of the children was the main problem in the marriage all by itself.

No child should ever be mistreated by a parent, whether it is a natural-born child or a stepchild or an adopted child; but both spouses made a covenant before God at the taking of their vows that they would put no one above their relationship with their spouse save the Lord. It is an unfortunate but very real truth that an ever-increasing number of families today are the result of two divorced parents marrying someone else, thus creating a totally new family structure which may bring children into a family situation in which the children were not born to one of the spouses. In these situations, there is also a great likelihood that some or all of the children may harbor resentment toward the new spouses of their birth parents. However, it is incumbent upon all husbands and wives – *before* they enter into a marriage covenant with each other – to stop and think about the fact that the most basic component of the marriage covenant is that they are agreeing to become one and cleave unto each other above *all* others. There are no exceptions in the marriage covenant for children who are already born prior to the marriage (or for anyone else, for that matter). Once a man and woman enter into a marriage covenant before God, they have necessarily committed their highest allegiance to each other above all others besides God. It is for this reason that divorced men and women should pray long and hard before making a decision to remarry if they already have children with someone else, especially minor children. No one should enter into a new marriage lightly without taking this important matter into account; for once the marriage is created, both husband and wife are bound by God to give each other their highest allegiance above all other humans, including their own children. If both adults being married are the kind of

Godly Christians that they should be, they will both love the children brought into the marriage by each other and will be able to navigate even through the difficult times which may arise; but there may still be struggles, especially with children who are not mature either emotionally or spiritually. This, of course, does not include any instances in which children are being abused; but absent abuse, there are no exceptions allowed for the wishes of the children in the marriage relationship. Once husband and wife covenant together before God, it makes no difference whether the children agree or do not agree, whether they like it or do not like it; the new husband and wife are bound by God to cleave unto each other and not allow anyone else, including their own children, to be given a higher allegiance than their own spouse. A husband or wife who gives a higher allegiance to their children than to their spouse has committed a breach of the marriage covenant before God and is just as guilty of destroying a marriage as someone who has committed adultery.

Case Study: Michele was a divorced mom of three. Her husband had given her Biblical grounds for a divorce – more than one, actually – so she was at liberty before God to remarry, provided that she chose a Godly man. She began seeing a man from church who loved God and was as involved in serving the Lord as she. The two fell in love, but her children constantly protested her seeing the man that she had begun seeing. They still harbored hopes that she would be reconciled to their father in spite of knowing that he had treated her wrongly. Quite honestly, these hopes of the children were more owing to their own selfish interests than anything. Each of the children had grown up somewhat spoiled and materialistic, and all were spiritually immature despite having grown up in church for the most part. Because of their immaturity, the deep bitterness of how their mom and dad's divorce had affected their own young lives and lifestyle was truly more of the reason that they

constantly protested against their mom seeing her new beau than even their hopes of their parents being reconciled. Nevertheless, Michele continued seeing the man from church, sometimes with her children's knowledge and oftentimes without them knowing. She was happy when she was with him. He made her feel alive again and not just romantically; she felt alive spiritually and rejoiced at having a partner who loved God as much as she.

Michele and her beau reached a point where they began to speak of marriage with each other. They discussed the exciting possibilities of a new life together but also the potential difficulties involving her children. Her new beau loved her children and treated them well; it was solely her children who did not feel the same about the relationship. Nevertheless, Michele finally reached a point at which she felt that she had peace from God to marry the man who had been courting her. He was pleasantly surprised when she shared the exciting news and cautioned her about being too hasty to make such a decision. Michele would not be deterred, however; and during a romantic weekend together while her children were with their father, she said that she was ready to be married... right then, right there. Again, her beau cautioned her lest she make a decision of which she was not truly certain, but she was extremely convincing; and he yielded to her. There was a very quiet ceremony with no guests present as the two made vows before God and were wed.

The couple was very happy about beginning their new life together after the weekend getaway. But then the weekend ended. As soon as Michele's children learned that their mother had eloped and gotten married, they refused to return and would not even agree to see or talk to their mother unless she divorced the man that she had just married. Although Michele knew that she was at liberty to remarry and had chosen a Godly man and knew that her own children had become increasingly worldly and fallen away from the Lord, her motherly instinct to have her children with her ripped her heart in two. Within weeks of the children's ultimatum, she left the man that she loved – her new husband – so that her children would still have something to do with her. Sadly, even after divorcing her beau that she said was "the man of her dreams" in order to have the acceptance of her children, her children still rarely spent time with her. They were off with friends or with their dad at his bigger home or always somewhere else.

This was a sad but perfect example of a spouse allowing someone (in this case, her own children) to come between her and her husband. She gave someone (her children) a higher allegiance than her husband to whom she owed it. Michele was not wrong for wanting her children's acceptance and certainly not for wanting them to spend time with her; it is what every good parent wants. She was wrong, however – in fact, in sin – for not cleaving unto her new husband and for allowing someone else to separate between them. It was the very opposite of what God commanded when He first created the institution of marriage for man in the Garden. Ironically, Michele ended up committing the same sin of breaching the marriage covenant that her first husband had committed against her. Though done for different reasons, she was nevertheless the guilty party before God when she ended her second marriage.

In the previous section on adultery, I tried to make clear that the Biblical ground of adultery is the actual physical act of adultery; however, this matter of "leaving and cleaving" also provides Biblical grounds for divorce when it involves the misappropriated affections that belong exclusively to a spouse. Legally, this is referred to as "alienation of affections" and does not require that any physical act of adultery has taken place. Although most states have done away with their laws which allow for civil cases to be brought using this legal concept, several states even today still allow it; and the concept is still acknowledged in divorce proceedings in all fifty states. Alienation of affections is precisely the Biblical grounds for divorce of which we are speaking when we talk about "leaving and cleaving," although it may involve a usurpation of other rights and privileges besides love, itself.

The two previous case studies that we have reviewed in this section have dealt with examples which did not involve romantic relationships, but romantic relationships probably make up the majority of cases in which there are Biblical grounds for divorce which fall into this category. One such example follows below and is solely intended as a sample; but the possible scenarios in this regard are endless.

Case Study: Frank and Betsy had a good marriage, a couple of children, and a comfortable home. The two had been married for nearly twenty years when Frank began to get bored with what he perceived to be the "routine" of the marriage. All marriages become "routine" at some point, and this is not necessarily a bad thing; it is all in the way that the husband and wife choose to view it. In a positive way, it means that life is comfortable – something which everyone wants at some point in life. However, if both spouses do not intentionally work to keep the romantic area of the relationship fresh, this can become a pitfall.

In this instance, Frank had a wife who loved him and still doted on him regularly. He certainly had no Biblical grounds for divorce and, quite honestly, had no lack of affection from his dear wife. It was his own yielding to temptations which was his problem: temptations from listening to the wrong kind of music, watching the wrong things on television, and associating with others at work who did not have a Biblical worldview. All of these subtly introduced a worldly

philosophy into his thinking that had not been there previously.

Quite out of the blue one day, Frank's routine interaction with an unmarried co-worker at the office seemed to create a spark between him and his co-worker, Miranda. There was nothing even romantic about the exchange, but both noticed a slight interest on the part of the other which soon grew into flirtation. There was still nothing physical to the relationship, but Frank had clearly crossed the line of what was appropriate since he was married. This new flirtatious relationship at the office became the central focus of his day; and he spent much of the day thinking about the next opportunity to accidentally "run into" Miranda around the office just to get to have a conversation and some more light flirting.

Betsy began to notice a change in Frank at home. He still did the routine things around the house but showed no interest in having more than a simple conversation with her about anything; and when he did, it was more of a business discussion than a familiar one. He stopped showing affection to Betsy and had little to no interest in the physical act of marriage, either. Betsy knew that something was wrong and worked overtime to please him and dote on him; but still nothing changed. Frank was a different person at work, all smiles and laughs, even when he wasn't interacting with Miranda.

Frank had clearly misappropriated the affection that, by virtue of the covenant that he made when he married Betsy, belonged exclusively to his wife. He had and was continuing to give to another something that did not belong to anyone but his spouse.

It is important to note in the above case study that not only had Frank broken his marriage covenant with Betsy by giving the affections that rightly belonged to her to another; but he had done so for no reason other than his own giving in to sinful temptations. Betsy had done nothing wrong, still loved him and loved on him, and had done nothing to give him any Biblical grounds to consider leaving. He was the sole spouse in the marriage who was in the wrong and in sin.

I have seen a number of instances over the years, however, when a spouse misappropriated their affections for a third party because the other spouse had either already done the same or had given some other Biblical grounds for divorce. This type of reciprocal sin is still wrong and is never the right course of action for a believer. God holds everyone – but especially believers – to a higher standard of conduct. He expects the believer to remain faithful within the marriage covenant as long as he or she is married. The believer must, then, make a choice: if the spouse has acted in such a way as to give legitimately Biblical grounds for divorce, then the believer may choose to divorce and separate or to forgive and remain. If the believer chooses to remain, for whatever reason, however, God expects the believer to maintain fidelity to the marriage covenant as long as he or she remains in it. This is precisely the reason that God allows even believers to have recourse to divorce upon certain grounds. He will allow a spouse to divorce for Biblical grounds, but He will not allow a spouse to act badly just because the other spouse does so. In that case, both spouses are in sin and at fault. The believer who has Biblical grounds must make a decision about divorcing or remaining in the marriage; there is no room for playing loose with the responsibilities to the marriage covenant if one chooses to remain in it. In such cases, it is better to divorce and depart for both conscience and testimony sake.

Even though a violation of the Biblical command for spouses to "leave and cleave" is not the same violation as the physical act of adultery, it is, nevertheless Biblical grounds for divorce because it is a breach of the marriage covenant.

Biblical Ground #4: Constructive Abandonment

Most states recognize another form of abandonment as legal grounds for divorce other than physical abandonment; this is known as constructive abandonment and occurs when a spouse ceases contributing to the marriage what he or she has covenanted to provide. The things which a spouse may cease contributing could include material things or physical intimacy or both; but the basic premise is that the things which are supposed to be provided to the other party are no longer being provided.

In today's modern, secular society, courts are less enthusiastic about identifying certain responsibilities in a marriage as belonging to either the husband or the wife, respectively. In previous times, of course, this was not so much the case. In our grandparents' generation, roles within marriage were still very traditional and very clearly delineated. The modern rise of feminism and egalitarianism in our society has continuously eroded the traditional Biblical view of the roles of husbands and wives. Nevertheless, in God's view, husbands and wives still have the same responsibilities that He established with the first marriage in the Garden; and men and women have very distinct roles and things for which they are responsible to provide in a Biblical marriage. As we have noted previously, this does not mean that there is no overlap of these things; nor does it mean that husbands and wives should not help each other with the burdens and mundane responsibilities of everyday life.

The things which husbands and wives are expected to contribute in their respective roles Biblically may be easily found in Scripture, beginning in the Garden. For the man, God commanded, as a result of his original sin, that he would have to work by the sweat of his brow to bring forth food; that is, the man is responsible to provide the basic needs of food, clothing, and shelter in the marriage. In bygone days, this was jokingly referred to as the husband "bringing home the bacon." It has traditionally been viewed as man's responsibilities, primarily, to provide these basic needs for his wife. In Bible days, the expectation for this was even more so in the cultures of the day. Today, with the advent of the women's liberation movement in culture and the intentional interferences in our economy that have created the need for two-income households, it is not necessarily viewed as the husband's role exclusively to provide these things; however, we know that Biblically God still holds the husband ultimately responsible for providing these things for his wife. Otherwise, if he is not able to provide these things for a wife, he should not take a wife since he is accepting responsibility to provide these things for her... both to God and to her daddy who is asked to give her hand in marriage.

Likewise, the wife has role-specific things for which she is responsible to provide in a marriage Biblically. These things, too, are easily found in Scripture beginning in the Garden. She is to be the primary spouse involved in both childbearing and child rearing. Again, this does not mean that dads should not care for their children and be involved in their raising; it simply means that moms are intentionally selected by God to be nurturing and to devote themselves to this task more so than husbands. It is also worth recognizing at this point, too, that, despite modern culture's views to the contrary, there is no higher calling for a woman than to be a good wife and a good mother; this is a noble calling and worthy of praise the Bible says in Proverbs 30. Wives are also called to be help meets for their husbands, that is to provide the support needed to assist their husbands in pursuing the callings that God has placed upon them. This has traditionally meant that wives have accepted the primary responsibility for taking care of the home by cooking, cleaning, and caring for the children.

It is possible, then, for a husband to remain physically present within the marriage while still "constructively" abandoning his marriage responsibilities. He can do this by ceasing to provide food, clothing, shelter, or medical care for his wife or by ceasing to fulfill his obligations to meet her intimate needs both physically, mentally, emotionally, and spiritually. The wife, likewise, may also remain physically present within the marriage while abandoning her responsibilities. A wife who refuses to cook, clean, care for the children, or fulfill her obligations to her husband's intimate needs from a mate are all examples of ways that wives may constructively abandon the marriage.

In Biblical times, God addressed the possibility of this kind of Biblical grounds for divorce in Exodus 21:10. The passage specifically addressed men who married a second wife while he was still married to his first wife. Although we do not allow polygamy in our society today (and God never condoned it either, by the way), the principle that is established in this passage is still valid for today, namely that a husband could not diminish the way that he provided for his wife. He was still expected to provide for her food, clothing, shelter, health, physical intimacy, and whatever other needs that she had at the same level as his new wife and, by implication, to provide for her at the same level that he provided for himself. The verse says plainly, *"If he take him another wife; her food, her raiment, and her duty of marriage, shall he not diminish."*

The next verse then goes on to tell us that if her husband does not provide these things, he is commanded to allow her to leave and to have her liberty once again: *"And if he do not these three unto her, then shall she go out free without money."* This is one of the instances in Scripture where divorce is actually *commanded*. The word "shall" is the same as "will," which means that in the case that the husband diminishes any of his obligations to his wife, the Bible says that she is to be set free (from the marriage covenant) and have her liberty to remarry restored. Notice, too, that it does not require that the husband completely cease providing these things for her in order for her to have Biblical grounds for divorce; it only requires that he diminishes the way that he provides for her, treating her as less than a wife.

Case Study: After several years of marriage, Eric was making a bit more money from work than previously. He routinely made impulse purchases of things related to his favourite hobbies including a new bass boat, new golf clubs on a regular basis, and a new firearm every few months. He reasoned that it was, after all, *his* **money that he was spending, so no one, including his wife Sharon should have a right to complain about it. Sharon tried not to broach the problem whenever possible because she had learned over time what Eric's response would be time and time again; sometimes it was unavoidable, however. She, too, worked outside the home; but because they had married young, she had never finished college because of raising their children, resulting in her bringing home substantially less than Eric every two weeks. In addition to putting gas in her vehicle and paying her car payment and insurance each month, Eric also expected her to buy groceries for the family out of her checks each month. Although Sharon did not think that it was fair, she continued to pay for her auto expenses or she would not have been able to get around or even get to work; and she continued to buy groceries with her paychecks since there would have been no food in the house if she did not. Meanwhile, Eric routinely blew extra money on unnecessary items each month and then refused to give Sharon money for basic necessities such as deodorant, co-pay for her to have an annual medical checkup, and other similar things, even when she did not have enough money to get those basic things because of having to buy groceries to make sure that the family was fed each month.**

This is a situation in which Eric clearly had ceased providing for even his wife's most basic needs and was providing for her in a different manner than he provided for himself.

While the passage in Exodus 21 deals with husbands abandoning their obligations under the marriage covenant, it is equally possible for wives to do the same. While some of the material obligations owed by husbands and wives may differ, wives nonetheless still have duties to which they are obligated under the covenant; and their ceasing – or even diminishing – to provide these things owed to their husbands constitutes Biblical grounds for divorce. A wife may not diminish the performance of her obligations to her husband without committing the same sin.

Case Study: When Marianne and Robert married, they both agreed that, as Christians, they wanted a traditional home which included Marianne being a stay-at-home mom when children were eventually born. Marianne worked outside the home for the first few years of the marriage until their son was born; but a few months prior to giving birth, she resigned her position as a pre-school teacher with plans to be a full-time housewife and mommy. For more than a year after the baby was born, she was the picture of a happy housewife both at home and out and about. She kept a neat house and even learned how to cook dishes that she had always wanted to learn.

However, after about a year, Marianne gradually began to become more and more undisciplined in both her household duties and her own personal habits. She began to routinely spend the day lying around the house watching soap operas or out shopping instead of caring for their home. She stopped making the bed, stopped cleaning like she always had, stopped doing the laundry, and stopped having anything prepared to eat when Robert got home from work each day. She even admitted that she had resorted to putting the baby in his playpen after getting him up each day and was pretty much leaving him to himself while she "watched her soaps." Robert, meanwhile, was left to do the laundry, himself, if he wanted to have clean clothes to wear to work and also had to fend for himself in the kitchen to find something to eat when he got home.

Concerned about his wife's obvious change in maintaining their home, Robert asked Marianne if she was having second thoughts about staying home instead of working outside the home; but her answer was always the same. She was absolutely not interested in going back to work... but neither did she seem to intend to do the things around the house to contribute like she had previously been doing. Eventually, Robert was brought to the point of having to broach the subject of her neglect of her duties around the house while he was away at work during the day. The conversations did not go well. Marianne was determined not to go back to work outside the home because Robert had promised her that she would not have to do so when they began to have children; but she also seemed just as determined to live the life of luxury without contributing around the house either.

This is a clear situation in which, as far as Robert knew, there was no infidelity on the part of his wife; but she had clearly stopped performing her own obligations in the marriage and contributing with an equal effort. The couple, like most, could not afford a maid and a cook; and Robert was now doing a great portion of her share of the workload around the home in addition to working his job during the day. Marianne grew more and more tired of the repeated conversations about her lack of work around the house and her apparent lack of motivation; and, consequently, she began "having headaches" whenever Robert tried to initiate intimate time together.

Marianne's failure to contribute equally to the marriage in a variety of areas was a breach of her marital obligations. Her justification to herself and to Robert was always that she was not being unfaithful and having an affair; but the reality is that she had, nonetheless, committed constructive abandonment; for though she was still physically present and not being unfaithful to Robert romantically, she was not upholding her responsibilities as a party to the marriage covenant.

As with other things that we have seen already, the principle of constructive abandonment should not be stretched to the absurd. For example, a husband or wife who is prevented from providing physical intimacy because of a health or medical situation is not necessarily voluntarily choosing to avoid the intimate obligations of marriage. So, too, would be the example of a wife who, because of health reasons, is not able to cook or clean like she would do otherwise. Similarly, a husband who is temporarily without work or is forced to take a job that pays less than he previously made is not necessarily intentionally diminishing the performance of his obligations in providing for his wife.

All marriages experience ups and downs financially over the course of a lifetime; and most of them also experience health issues with one or both spouses at different times, as well, especially as age increases. Having less to offer each other materially does not implicitly mean that there is a breach of the marriage covenant on the part of either spouse. This is what is meant by wedding vows that include the words "for richer or for poorer, in sickness and in health." There is no guarantee that a certain level of prosperity must be maintained. What is expected is that both spouses are sincerely working to perform their obligations to their spouses without being lazy or undisciplined and that both spouses are treating each other at least as well as they are treating themselves.

Biblical Ground #5: Financial Slavery

Marriages among unbelievers – and in some cases, among believers – take place for a multitude of reasons nowadays. One of those reasons is sometimes for financial gain; and while it may be that both spouses see the economic advantages of having a partner in the goals of life, I am speaking now more of the scenario in which one or the other spouse is choosing to marry or remain married primarily because of the financial gain to be had at the expense of the other spouse. We have all heard the derogatory use of the term "gold digger" for women who are perceived as marrying for financial gain; but in the right situations, the same could apply to men, as well.

In Deuteronomy 21:14, God gives specific prohibitions against keeping a spouse primarily for financial gain. In context, the passage is dealing with men of Israel who took women captive during battle with their enemies and then forced them into marriage. Today, our society does not openly allow any such behaviour, even during times of war; but this does not mean that there aren't still marriages which have ultimately the same resulting and degrading effects. The verse specifically states: *"but thou shalt not sell her at all for money, thou shalt not make merchandise of her, because thou hast humbled her."* God tells the men of Israel that they were not permitted to keep wives for the primary purpose of financial gain. In other words, they were forbidden to keep a wife as a financial slave instead of treating her as a "wife" was to be treated. They could neither sell her for her labour nor for sexual acts. She must be treated with all of the respect and love to which wives are entitled in the marriage covenant (i.e., her husband putting her interests before his own).

Today, both men and women, both believers and unbelievers, are guilty of committing this same sin. They either marry for financial gain or they remain in a marriage for financial gain; but because the financial gain is the primary motivation, they fail to treat their spouses in the loving and respectful way that is demanded by God within marriage. Women sometimes marry or remain in marriages because they like the lifestyle that comes with being married to a successful man in the business world; and men sometimes marry or remain in marriages because they do not wish to shoulder the financial burdens of life without someone else to help "pay the bills." When this becomes the primary reason for marrying or staying married, it is a clear violation of the command that God gave to the children of Israel in Deuteronomy 21:14.

Case Study: Jonathan and Elise married right out of high school. They both worked outside of the home and both improved their job situations over the years to the point that they were making a comfortable living together. They not only were able to take vacations several times a year but also had managed to have a large house, nice cars, a boat, an RV, a swimming pool, and more. Unfortunately, like too many couples today, most of what they "bought" was purchased on credit; and it took both of their incomes every month just to keep the bills current, especially due to the interest that they paid on everything.

As time went on, Jonathan more and more seemed disinterested in Elise. Oh, he never abused her physically, mind you; but he showed little regard for her, her values (which used to be his own, as well, or so he had said when they married), or her desires. After more than a few years of the same kind of treatment, Elise announced one day that she was leaving him and filing for divorce. Jonathan immediately went to his pastor to beg for help to "save his marriage." Very telling, though, were the next words out of his mouth to the preacher, "She can't go, she just can't. How will I even be able to pay the bills? I'll lose the house!" He

then followed that statement with another which was just as telling, "And I'll never be able to find someone else that will want to marry me." Though his comments were made with tears and though he followed those comments with declarations of his love for Elise, the first words that had come out of his mouth sent up red flags for his pastor. The pastor, like most people, expected the first words out of his mouth to be something along the lines of "She just can't leave. I love her." But, alas, his first words showed the true primary motives that he had in keeping her in the marriage. Everything that he said afterwards just seemed like a child who says whatever is necessary in order to get his way.

Still, hoping to help the couple save their marriage, the pastor spent months counseling and spending time with the couple in an effort to help restore their marriage. Each time that Elise would again threaten to leave because Jonathan's change was short-lived, Jonathan would plead with her not to go, often with tears; but each time, his pleading always included the argument that she couldn't go because neither of them could make it on their own financially. He said that "they didn't even have two nickels to rub together" between the two of them because they were so in debt for the things that they had already purchased on credit.

More and more it became apparent that, in spite of his words to the contrary, Jonathan's primary desire to keep Elise in the marriage was derived from his view of the financial profit and loss sheet rather than love for his wife. It was clearly a modern case of Deuteronomy 21:14. Elise was not taken captive in war, and she was not forced at gunpoint to marry him; but she was, nonetheless, treated as a financial slave exactly as it was prohibited by God in the passage. In effect, Jonathan had consistently tried to use the couple's debts as a way to keep his wife imprisoned in a

marriage where she was not treated properly. What a cruel device his use of marriage had become!

In God's prohibition to the men of Israel against keeping a wife as a financial slave, He also stated clearly what was to be done in that situation: "then thou shalt let her go whither she will." God gave the wife liberty to divorce her husband in this situation; and He commanded the husband to grant the divorce if the wife asked for it. God's view of the marriage covenant is not that of a financial investment; but, rather, it is of a loving relationship on the part of both parties... and He does not allow either party to be held captive or abused for the selfish motives of the other party.

Biblical Ground #6: Having no Delight In

This Biblical ground for divorce is very closely related to the one that we just discussed; in fact, it is found in the exact same verses that we've already seen. But I have intentionally listed it separately on purpose because there is a distinction between the two. Deuteronomy 21:14 says, *"And it shall be, if thou have no delight in her, then thou shalt let her go whither she will; but thou shalt not sell her at all for money, thou shalt not make merchandise of her, because thou hast humbled her."* Again, this is speaking of the men of Israel taking wives of captives in war. If the men did this, they were required by God to treat these wives the way that God tells us repeatedly in Scripture that husbands are to treat their wives. They could not be treated as lesser than other wives or treated as financial slaves by the husband.

So what is meant when the Bible says, "if thou have no delight in her?" This speaks of the husband not having feelings towards his wife like he is supposed to have for his wife. We have already discussed what this relationship is supposed to be like in the first part of this book; but in a nutshell, he is to love his wife as himself and to put her best interests above his own. He is to treat her like a precious treasure, not as property and not as a slave. If a husband does not have delight in his wife, it means that he no longer wishes to treat her as his wife... for whatever reason.

I have distinguished this Biblical ground for divorce from the preceding one even though they are both mentioned in the same verse for this reason: all husbands who treat their wives as financial slaves "take no delight" in their wives, but not all husbands who "take no delight" in their wives go so far as to treat their wives as financial slaves. You see, it is possible for a husband to simply disregard his wife, push her away and want nothing to do with her, without using her for financial gain. Either way, however, the husband is in the wrong; and it leaves the wife trapped in a relationship that is less than what God intended the marriage relationship to be. God is not so cruel as to demand that any wife be imprisoned in a marriage where she is not loved and where she is not treated as a wife is to be treated. Likewise, however, wives may not treat their husbands in this manner without breaching the marriage covenant, themselves.

During both the Old Testament period and the New Testament, there were men in Israel who were misconstruing this command from God that had been given to Moses. The men of Israel were saying, "See, the Mosaic Law said that if we have no delight in our wives, we can divorce them." Consequently, when they found women that struck their fancy, they would divorce their existing wives and marry the new ones. This was precisely what Jesus was addressing in the New Testament when He told them in Matthew 19:9, *"And I say unto you, Whosoever shall put away his wife, except it be for fornication, and shall marry another, committeth adultery."* He was not saying that there were no other Biblical grounds for divorce, even under the law. Rather, He was saying that they could not just throw away their wives unless the wives had committed adultery. He was condemning their practice of divorcing their wives just because they were tired of them and then using the law as their justification.

So then, Deuteronomy 21:14 is not giving husbands permission to just throw away their wives, as the men of Israel were doing; it is, rather, prohibiting them from treating their wives as less than wives are to be treated. But if, in the hardness of their hearts and their rebellion against God, the husbands are still bound and determined to try to force their wives to stay even though they no longer delight in them, God commands the husbands to allow their wives to leave; and He restores the liberty to marry another to the wives who have been thus treated. Perhaps ironically, it is the wives in these situations who had the Biblical grounds for divorce, not the husbands who argued that they did.

Case Study: Richard and Lisa had a good marriage for seven years until Richard seemed to begin to lose interest in both Lisa and their marriage. He constantly found things about which to complain, and most of them had something to do with Lisa or with the way that she did things. Not only did he complain, but he also routinely made jokes at her expense or made comments about her physical appearance that were unnecessary. On one occasion, he made a "joke" about her teeth not being straight in front of a group of church members; and, although he did it under the guise of a "funny joke," he knew very well how self-conscious Lisa was about the fact that she did not have perfect teeth like some of the other wives with whom they associated because she had shared her anxiety about it in private with him numerous times over the years. He continued to find faults with his wife and to voice them, both in public and in private. He constantly worked overtime and then spent hours on his hobbies in an apparent effort to get out of spending time with Lisa. He avoided intimate time with her whenever possible and then claimed he was too tired when he couldn't avoid the subject any other way. Over the course of time, Richard even began making comments to Lisa about how attractive other women were, including some of her own friends, all while continuing to show disdain and disinterest in his own wife. She repeatedly tried to talk with him about all of the problems and his own apparent lack of interest; but he was never willing to talk about his "feelings" or anything important that had to do with their relationship. He was fine talking about such factual things as the bills and what to eat for dinner; but when it came to talking about their relationship, he made it understood by his lack of interest that he had no desire to talk about their relationship, let alone improve it. While Richard had not yet crossed the line into physical adultery, his long pattern of behaviour showed that he no longer took any delight in his

wife; and while he had no Biblical grounds for divorce, she clearly did.

The long and short of the principle is this: husband do not have Biblical grounds to divorce their wives just because the husband falls out of love with his wife. The wife, however, does have Biblical grounds for divorce if her husband begins to treat her as though he is no longer in love with her (no longer "delights" in her). And this is true in reverse for wives, also. You may not divorce your spouse just because you "fall out of love" with him or her, otherwise *you* are in direct disobedience to God. But if you begin to treat your spouse as less than you should in marriage, *your spouse* has Biblical grounds for divorce — not you, but your spouse. *You are still in the wrong*, but *they* have Biblical grounds to depart because of your sin.

Biblical Ground #7: Withholding the Act of Marriage

The physical act of marriage is an integral part of the marriage relationship. It is the consummation of the husband and wife becoming one; for during the act of marriage, the two literally become one flesh as we have seen from Scripture. The withholding of this marital privilege by either spouse, then, is a serious matter which can become a breach in the marriage covenant all by itself.

In I Corinthians 7, beginning in verse 2, the Apostle Paul says, "Nevertheless, *to avoid* fornication, let every man have his own wife, and let every woman have her own husband. Let the husband render unto the wife due benevolence: and likewise also the wife unto the husband. The wife hath not power of her own body, but the husband: and likewise also the husband hath not power of his own body, but the wife. Defraud ye not one the other, except *it be* with consent for a time, that ye may give yourselves to fasting and prayer; and come together again, that Satan tempt you not for your incontinency."

This passage to the church in Corinth is teaching several things. Firstly, being married and having an intimate partner within the marriage covenant is preferable to committing fornication. Secondly, in marriage, the husband's body belongs to his wife; and the wife's body belongs to her husband. Therefore, thirdly, husbands and wives should not withhold physical intimacy from their spouses ("defraud ye not") because such action inevitably opens one or both spouses to temptation to commit adultery.

Paul does, however, acknowledge that withholding from the physical act of intimacy within marriage is permitted but only with certain rules: 1) There must be consent; that is, both spouses must be in agreement about withholding. 2) It must only be for a specified period of time, never an open-ended arrangement to simply stop having intimate relations indefinitely. 3) And lastly, it should only be for the purpose of praying and fasting about some important matter. In this instance, withholding from the pleasure of physical intimacy is tied to the principle of withholding from the pleasure of eating because whatever is being prayed about is so important that the participants desire for God to see their acknowledgment of their need for His divine intervention.

Any married couple which allows themselves to stop having physical marital relations have set themselves up for temptation and potential disaster, not only for the sake of their marriage but for their individual lives, as well. Few women, and perhaps even fewer men, have the wherewithal to not yield to temptation if their intimate needs are not being met by their spouses. Even if the temptations do not result in the physical act of adultery, they will doubtless result in lust and immoral thoughts about others outside of the marriage relationship at the very least.

As Paul states in I Corinthians 7, our bodies within marriage belong to our spouse; and we do not have authority to withhold physical intimacy from our spouses. The physical act, itself, is a marital right and one which is a fundamental part of the very covenant. Once a husband and wife become "one flesh," they both have the right to expect that physical relations will be an ongoing, regular occurrence. For this reason, any spouse who voluntarily withholds the right of physical intimacy from his or her spouse for a prolonged or open-ended period of time is in breach of the marriage contract; and the other spouse has Biblical grounds for divorce.

Unfortunately, husbands and wives all too often use the withholding of physical intimacy as a weapon against their mates during times of disagreement. They literally weaponize one of the greatest joys of marriage. Withholding love, forgiveness, or physical affection in a marriage that is still whole is a good way to kill it.

Case Study: Barbara and Ryan were a middle-aged couple who had been married to each other for about five years. For the most part, they enjoyed a good relationship with each other and with others. Barbara, however, was not exactly the picture of a model submissive wife as described in the Bible; she was very vocal of her opinions, even when she publicly disagreed with Ryan about things. Though she was very intelligent, Barbara was also as moody as she was opinionated; and no one, including Ryan ever knew which mood to expect. It was generally one extreme or another. Barbara also had another very bad habit: each time she had a disagreement with Ryan or did not get her way about something, she would refuse to have marital relations. She did not just momentarily withhold physical intimacy during the disagreements, themselves; it was not uncommon for her to go an entire week in this manner after such a disagreement. It was very clear that she was making a point and that she intended to "punish" her husband even if he "won" the disagreement. She was much like the spoiled child in the grocery store who lies down in the floor, screaming and pitching a fit, because he doesn't get the toy in the checkout line that he wants.

The problem had existed since early on in their five year marriage; but Ryan had managed to cope with it even though he knew it was wrong and unBiblical. That all changed one autumn day, however, when the two sat down after supper to discuss a job offer than Ryan had received. A business competitor of Ryan's employer had reached out to him and offered him a substantial salary increase if he would change companies. The added income would definitely have given Ryan and Barbara enough expendable income that they could have significantly improved their standard of living; but the job offer came with a caveat... Ryan would have to work most Saturdays and occasional evenings in addition to his customary hours. The couple already had a comfortable living, and all of the bills were paid each month with money left over; so Ryan was not so eager to accept the offer. He enjoyed spending time at home with Barbara and working outside in their garden. He also enjoyed participating in the extra activities that the church had for men and for couples. Barbara, though, could not believe that he was actually considering turning down an opportunity for so much more money every month. The two discussed the matter for nearly a week before Ryan eventually declined the job offer with the other company. The competitor told him that if he changed his mind, the offer would still be open. Barbara said with her mouth that she agreed it was his choice to make; but she said something far different with her actions in the privacy of their home. She set about to get him to change his mind by immediately withholding the physical act of marriage; and she continued this without abatement. Over time, even others around the couple could tell that there was something wrong between the two; but out of respect for his wife and what he believed was right, Ryan never told anyone of Barbara's private behaviour. Barbara was determined to continue until Ryan caved in to her demand to accept the better-paying job. This continued for nearly four months until Ryan approached his pastor seeking counseling. When Ryan confided in his pastor enough for the pastor to have an understanding of what was going on, the pastor requested a meeting with both spouses to try to get their marriage back on track. Both spouses showed up together for the counseling, and Barbara even admitted that Ryan's story was basically true; but when the pastor shared with her that her approach to get her husband to change his mind about the job was unScriptural, she brazenly stated that it was "her body" and that she would not be resuming normal marital relations until she was good and ready. She then left the session and waited for her husband in the car. Their pastor promised Ryan that he would continue to pray for them both and that he would still meet with one or both of them if they were willing; but Barbara was determined not to return to counseling with a "man" because, in her words, he simply took her husband's side without concern for her feelings as a woman. Barbara continued her behaviour for several more months after which Ryan filed for a divorce. She seemed surprised that he would take that step even though he had tried to tell her repeatedly that he intended to do so if things didn't change. She refused to change right up to the end, always asserting that she would resume normal relations once he changed his mind and followed her advice about taking the other job. At that point, it had actually become more about pride and "winning" the issue to Barbara than it was about what was right and wrong... or even about the extra income. Even when the divorce was finalized, she steadfastly maintained that she had a right to withhold intimacy with "her body" if she wanted. She was wrong, for the Bible clearly teaches that husbands and wives do not have the right to withhold physical intimacy from each other indefinitely for any reason and certainly not for selfish reasons.

Headaches, though, do occur in real life; and whether it's a headache or some other medical issue, there are times when one or both spouses may need a pause in physical intimacy purely owing to health reasons. If this genuinely occurs – and is not merely an excuse for withholding it for some ulterior motive – love, compassion, and understanding on the part of both spouses must be the rule of the day. Situations in which a spouse cannot participate in physical intimacy because of a medical condition should not be lumped into the same category as someone stubbornly refusing to have physical intimacy for some selfish reason. If this kind of situation occurs – and it does occur every day – it is imperative that both spouses have a loving and selfless approach toward each other concerning this matter; and, even though some states acknowledge the absence of physical intimacy due to medical conditions as legal grounds for divorce, it is not a Biblical ground for divorce absent any other Biblical grounds.

Being loving and sensitive to one's spouse, though, is essential in exercising the right of physical intimacy in marriage. Just because God tells us that we have a right to this gift from our spouse does not mean that any given moment is a time that we should choose to exercise it. Although intentionally withholding physical intimacy because of anger or not getting one's way may be wrong, so, too, can be the attempt to exercise this right at the wrong time. No one wants to feel that they are forced to give physical intimacy when things are not right between them and their partner; this feels too eerily similar to something that all decent people stand against. Intimacy between spouses should always be accompanied by love and selflessness. If these things are not present at any given time, whatever needs to be done to first remedy this problem should happen before anyone seeks to exercise their marital rights, whether it be sitting down and discussing problems or being forthcoming with an apology if one is owed for something. When genuinely accompanied by tenderness, love, and selflessness, the physical act of marriage can provide a good balm to help both spouses feel as one again after having a disagreement as long as the disagreement has already been dealt with in a Biblical manner.

Biblical Ground #8: Fraud

According to Black's Law Dictionary, any activity which relies on deception in order to achieve a gain constitutes fraud; and it becomes criminal whenever a material fact is knowingly misrepresented or withheld in order to get another to act to his detriment. God is no more accepting of fraud than man is. Fraud perpetrated by a would-be husband or wife in order to get the other party to marry can provide Biblical grounds for divorce or, more correctly, can void the marriage covenant as though it never existed in the first place.

Before we go any further in dealing with this subject, it is important that we clarify that the kind of fraud of which we are speaking is one that deals with a matter of a serious nature; that is, we are not speaking of fraud related to any trivial issues. For example, a groom-to-be who lies and tells his bride-to-be that he cannot recall the name of his first girlfriend from kindergarten may be fraud, but it does not rise to the level of being Biblical grounds for divorce. Similarly, a bride-to-be who tells her soon-to-be husband that she has never kissed anyone else before but intentionally "forgets" that she kissed the boy who escorted her to the homecoming football game in 9th grade may be committing fraud; but, again, the severity of the fraud does not rise to the level of Biblical grounds for divorce.

In order for fraud to constitute Biblical grounds for divorce, it must be a matter which is grave enough that it necessarily alters the arrangement into which both husband and wife believe they are entering. As we have previously discussed in this book, a marriage is a contract between husband and wife; and, like all legal contracts, the parties entering into the contract have a right to know up front what the terms of the contract are, as well as any pre-existing conditions which might affect the performance of the contract. Businessmen entering into a contract together, for example, do not have a right to know what kind of shampoo each other uses; but they do have a right to know if each other is engaged in any other business activity which may in some way negatively affect their current business venture together. In short, if the detail may affect their business arrangement together, both parties are obligated to divulge the information to each other and to be truthful about it. This hearkens back to the legal definition of fraud that we saw from Black's Legal Dictionary: a party who either misrepresents *or* withholds relevant information which keeps the other party from being able to have a clear and accurate picture of the arrangement and any possible entanglements prior to signing the contract is committing fraud against his partner. This is because each party to the contract has a right to have a clear and accurate picture of what he is getting himself into *before* he signs the contract.

Notice from the legal definition of fraud that it may include either a misrepresentation of material facts or merely the withholding of material facts. What are material facts? These are facts which are significant enough that they have the ability to either alter the relationship between the parties in the contract or to alter the value of the contract to one or both parties. In other words, if something might make the contract less attractive to the second party, the first party has an obligation to make the second party aware of it beforehand so that the second party can make a voluntary decision as to whether it will change the agreement enough to make it no longer an arrangement into which he wishes to enter. Let's face it, little things might be no big deal, especially if one knows about them in advance; but no one likes to be caught off guard with major surprises... either in business arrangements or in marriages. It is precisely these kind of major things that could constitute fraud. A good question to ask when trying to decide whether something is important enough to rise to this level of significance is this: "Does this fact have the potential to change the value of the deal to the other party? Or, perhaps more simply put, is this something that the other person would want to know before deciding if he or she wants to enter into this arrangement?"

We all have things that we are uncomfortable talking about with others, especially if we think that it may change that person's desire to have whatever kind of relationship with us that we wish to have with that other person. And if we are merely talking about golfing buddies, there is one level of obligation to divulge facts; but when we are talking about someone with whom we are discussing making a lifetime marriage commitment to become "one," there is a totally different level of obligation to be forthcoming with important facts.

Misrepresentation of facts and the withholding of facts are both fair game for what constitutes fraud. Most everyone can agree that a misrepresentation of facts is fraud; after all, it's flat out lying, especially if it concerns something important. Even the very Ten Commandments tell us, *"Thou shalt not bear false witness."* This means we are not to lie. Many people, however, are reluctant to acknowledge that merely "withholding" information is in the same category as telling a lie. They seek to justify their withholding of information to others – and to themselves, I might add – by reasoning that they are not actually telling a falsehood... they just aren't bringing up things that they have not been asked. After all, they would argue, why should they be responsible for telling things that they haven't been asked? The other party could have asked the question if they really wanted to know... or so they convince themselves. The courts do not view these two things as different, though; and it is doubtful if God does either. We serve the One Who is *"the Way, the TRUTH, and the Life,"* after all. I'm pretty sure that He expects us to tell the truth, the whole truth, and nothing but the truth when it comes to being forthwith to our future mate. This includes sharing things that we know our partner has a right to know whether or not they have asked about it. To be completely honest, they may not even know there is anything to ask in a certain area, let alone what question to ask. The key is transparency. If it could possibly affect the other person's decision on whether they want to enter into marriage because of it, we have an obligation to make sure that they know whatever it is before we enter into that covenant.

One of the reasons for which business contracts may be declared null and void by the courts is if pertinent information was either misrepresented *or* withheld from one of the parties when the contract was originally signed. All parties must sign the contract voluntarily; and they must sign it with an accurate understanding of what they are signing. Even if it is in "fine print," the important stuff must be there in the contract in order for it to be enforceable after the fact. Now whether or not both parties read the fine print is up to them. And whether the other party regards the potentially significant information as important enough to reconsider the entire arrangement or not is up to that person; but he has that right. He *has* to have that right. Otherwise, he has been deceived, tricked into something that he might not would have otherwise agreed. He has that right, and you have that right... the right to know clearly what the situation is into which you are obligating yourself for life and *to whom* you are obligating yourself for life.

The Bible very specifically deals with one such example of fraud in Deuteronomy 22:13-21 which states: *"If any man take a wife, and go in unto her, and hate her, And give occasions of speech against her, and bring up an evil name upon her, and say, I took this woman, and when I came to her, I found her not a maid: Then shall the father of the damsel, and her mother, take and bring forth the tokens of the damsel's virginity unto the elders of the city in the gate: And the damsel's father shall say unto the elders, I gave my daughter unto this man to wife, and he hateth her; And, lo, he hath given occasions of speech against her, saying, I found not thy daughter a maid; and yet these are the tokens of my daughter's virginity. And they shall spread the cloth before the elders of the city. And the elders of that city shall take that man and chastise him; And they shall amerce him in an hundred shekels of silver, and give them unto the father of the damsel, because he hath brought up an evil name upon a virgin of Israel: and she shall be his wife; he may not put her away all his days. But if this thing be true, and the tokens of virginity be not found for the damsel: Then they shall bring out the damsel to the door of her father's house, and the men of her city shall stone her with stones that she die: because she hath wrought folly in Israel, to play the whore in her father's house: so shalt thou put evil away from among you."*

The passage above deals with the fraudulent claim of virginity. The significance of this issue should be obvious even in our own day and time; but it was even more so in the days in which the Bible was written. Purity mattered then. Purity should matter now. But the passage describes a situation in which a man marries a bride and then fraudulently claims that he discovered that she was not a virgin like he had been led to believe when they married. His reason for making this false claim is that he "hated" her – that is, he wasn't as fond of her after marrying her as he thought he was beforehand; so he made up a lie to get out of his marriage to her. The Mosaic Law gave a fairly accurate means of disproving such a claim by a lying husband: her parents would be given the bed linens from the honeymoon suite after the wedding night; and they would retain them as "proof" if ever the question arose about her virginity at the time of marriage. The significance of the bed linens was, of course, that if she were a virgin, there would be at least some amount of blood on the linens from having her hymen broken during the physical act of marriage for the first time. The absence of any blood at all could indicate that she was not a virgin. The significance of this passage for our discussion of Biblical grounds for divorce centers around the issue of fraud – more specifically, fraud which was perpetrated prior to the marriage covenant being made. Did the girl (and her parents) lie about her being a virgin or not? Was the husband presented something in the marriage contract which was a fraud (i.e., he didn't get what he was led to believe he was getting... a virgin bride)? The issue is significant enough that if it could be proven that the bride was not a virgin after she was put forth as one before marriage, the marriage was voided; and, worse yet for the girl, she was stoned to death in order to discourage impurity and fraud throughout Israel. If, however, her parents could demonstrate from the "tokens" of her virginity (i.e., the bloody bed linens from her wedding night) that she was, indeed, a virgin at the time of marriage, it was the lying husband who was punished. God is not pleased with impurity; and neither is He pleased with fraud perpetrated upon an innocent party. The husband had a right to believe that he was getting what he was told he was getting in his bride when he entered into the marriage covenant. Had he known that she was not a virgin, he could have decided not to marry her; it would have been his choice to make having all of the facts to consider. By the same token, wives are entitled to the same thing... honesty and transparency about what they are getting *beforehand*.

If the husband in the passage was defrauded, he was absolved of his obligation to the marriage. In fact, God did not even require divorce in this situation: He completely voided the contract as though it never existed when He commanded the stoning of the bride. Contracts which are predicated upon fraud are invalid from their outset, even if it should be some time down the road before the victim realizes that a fraud has been perpetrated upon him or her.

Notice, too, not only God's serious view of fraud but also His serious view of false accusations of fraud. If the husband in the passage was found to have lied about the girl not being a virgin, the husband was to be beaten and fined a substantial amount of money. Perhaps more interesting, though, is the fact that God said that because he sought to soil her good name by accusing her of whoredom, he was forbidden to divorce her for the rest of her life. What may not be obvious at first reading of this is the fact that, after lying about her character, he was now stuck with her for the rest of their lives and had to take care of her with no option for getting out even if he tried to invoke the much-abused grounds for divorce that we have already seen among the men of Israel by saying that he no longer "delighted" in her later on. This was off the table; and, although hopefully she would always have a sweet spirit about her as God would desire, her sorry husband was forbidden to divorce her even if he ended up with a wife who resented him for the rest of his life. Perhaps that was his greater punishment for lying about her reputation! By the way, although the passage says that *he* was forbidden to divorce *her* for the rest of their lives, it does not say that *she* was forbidden to divorce *him*; so, perhaps the Lord left the door open for her to still have a way out if she wished it, even though the door was nailed shut for him.

This passage clearly delineates at least one fraud which is so serious as to be able to completely void the entire marriage covenant as though it never existed – that is a false claim of virginity which is not so. To be honest, this is the only issue of fraud which the Bible mentions specifically. Some might argue that this is the only issue of fraud which voids a marriage covenant or serves as Biblical grounds for divorce since it entails sexual impurity – referred to as "playing the whore" in the passage. However, a thorough study of the Bible – even just the Old Testament context in which we find this – demonstrates otherwise. There are other instances in the Old Testament in which men married harlots; and God clearly recognized their marriages without declaring them null and void. Why? Because the marriages were made with the husbands having clear knowledge ahead of time of what they were getting when they married the wives that they married. The knew that their wives had previously been harlots, but they chose to marry them anyway. In these instances, the husbands did not have Biblical grounds for divorce after the fact because they knew what they were getting when they married; there was no fraud committed. One clear example of this would be the prophet Hosea who knowingly married a harlot. God used Hosea's marriage to Gomer to preach a series of messages to the nation of Israel... but God still regarded it as a marriage. Why? Because Hosea knew in advance of his bride-to-be's background and reputation. Another Israelite of the Old Testament who married a harlot was Salmon. You may not remember Salmon's name, but you likely are more familiar with the name of the woman that he married... Rahab of Jericho. A number of Bible expositors believe that Salmon was one of the two Israelite spies hidden in Jericho by Rahab; but whether this is the case or not, whoever Salmon was, he was clearly a Hebrew of the tribe of Judah, father of Boaz, and an ancestor of both King David and the human lineage of the Messiah. Both of these men married harlots, but God did not void their marriages. Why not? Because they both entered into the marriages with full knowledge of the "deal" that they were getting when they entered voluntarily into the contract.

Since in the passage in Deuteronomy God is not primarily voiding the marriage covenant because of the sin of harlotry, it leaves only the sin of fraud as the primary reason. The reason that the theoretical "husband" in the passage had his marriage annulled by God was because a fraud was perpetrated upon him. In modern terms, he was sold a false bill of goods. He was made to believe something about the bride-to-be that was not so. The Bible does not even go so far as to tell us whether the theoretical husband believed that his bride was a virgin because he was explicitly told this by the girl and her parents or because he implicitly assumed it because they did not divulge her indiscretions to him beforehand. It did not matter which was the case. In either case, it was fraud; because withholding material facts of substance of that magnitude was just as much a lie as deliberate misrepresentation. It was something that he was entitled to know before making a decision to enter into a lifetime commitment with her in marriage.

The fact that it was obviously the element of fraud that voided the marriage covenant, then, begs the question... what other matters constitute such a serious fraud that they are worthy of having a marriage covenant voided either through annulment or divorce? Again, the matters, whatever they may be, must be of such magnitude that they significantly alter the "deal" that the other party is getting in the marriage arrangement. Undoubtedly, some will argue that there are no other matters weighty enough to invalidate a marriage besides a false pronouncement of virginity before marriage since it is the only one explicitly given as an example in the Bible. Knowing the premium, however, that our God places upon truth, honesty, and forthrightness, it does not seem in keeping with His character that He would rubber stamp any form of significant fraud which created a false picture for one of the parties getting married even if it did not include a claim of virginity. The absence of other examples of matters that are of such significance specifically named in Scripture does not preclude the possibility – nor the probability – that others exist. The Bible rarely seeks to give an exhaustive list of every single possible sin, or even category of sin; but what it does is provide us with Biblical principles to apply... even to things which exist in modern society which did not in the first century or before. In this case, the principle is fraud in marriage.

Since the Bible does not provide such an exhaustive list of which matters are weighty enough to invalidate a marriage due to fraud, we must allow the Holy Spirit to guide us in applying the principles that we have already examined. I will no more attempt to create an exhaustive list of what those things might be than the Bible has done; but I will suggest a few items that may fall into this category along with the false claim of virginity before marriage so as to give an accurate view of the weightiness of which we are speaking. Here are just a few that I personally think may very well rise to that same level of gravity.

What if you discovered after being married that your spouse was... a convicted murderer? It's very possible in the day and time in which we live, with so many states allowing murderers to go free after serving a specified number of years behind bars.

What if you discovered after being married that your spouse was... a convicted child molester? Would you want to take a chance on bringing children into the world in a home where they may be victimized because you believed you were bound to that marriage covenant in spite of the fact that you did not know about it previously?

What if you discovered after being married that your spouse was... in debt, with numerous judgments against him or her? What if after marriage you learned this, probably after being declined for a home or a car or something else because of their wretched credit score? What if it was only after marriage that you came to the stark realization that you had married someone whose own financial past was destined to prevent you from ever having the future about which you had dreamed... and for which you had worked so hard your entire life up to that point? And what if you lived in one of the states which still allows creditors to go after the spouse's assets even if the debts belong to the other spouse?

What if you discovered after being married that your spouse was... not convicted but wanted for a crime?

What if you discovered after being married that your spouse was. infected with a highly communicable disease, especially one for which there is no known cure? And especially if it turned out to be especially communicable through intimacy?

What if you discovered after being married that your spouse was... mentally ill? Perhaps you discovered after marriage that your spouse had a history of mental illness, had perhaps even been institutionalized at some point.

What if you discovered after being married that your spouse was... someone with a mental or emotional illness which had unhealthy, dangerous, or disgusting side effects... and they refused to get help for them?

What if you discovered after being married that your spouse was. born a different gender; but because you followed the Biblical protocol and had no physical relations before marriage, you had no way of knowing that?

I fully realize that none of these issues are explicitly stated in the Bible as examples of fraud worthy of voiding a marriage; but they certainly seem to violate the Law of Contracts observed in both secular and Biblical realms which demand that 1) both parties enter into the covenant voluntarily and 2) both parties have an accurate understanding of the deal that they are getting in the contract before accepting it. Galatians 3:15 affirms that, even among mankind, this principle ordained by God is observed.

But if you're reading this book and you're still not comfortable with adding these and other similar things to the list of frauds because they are not mentioned along with virginity, as worthy of terminating a marriage, I would invite you to step back for a moment and consider these things from a different perspective. Instead of considering each of these possibilities as though YOU were the one deceived and subsequently trapped in a marriage after being defrauded in one or more of these examples, consider them for a moment as though it were YOUR CHILD who had been defrauded and subsequently found himself or herself trapped in such a marriage. This is a very legitimate consideration; for it is exactly the view from which God as our Heavenly Father would view these matters if it were us in these situations. And, again, knowing the character of our God, it does not seem reasonable that He would allow one of His own children to be imprisoned for life in a marriage in which His child was deceived, misled, tricked, lied to, or intentionally left untold about these serious things. He loves His children far too much to allow such injustice, I believe, when He, Himself, is a just God. This is a Biblical principle that we find in very plain language in Matthew 7: *"Or what man is there of you, whom if his son ask bread, will he give him a stone? Or if he ask a fish, will he give him a serpent? If ye then, being evil, know how to give good gifts unto your children, how much more shall your Father which is in heaven give good things to them that ask him? Therefore all things whatsoever ye would that men should do to you, do ye even so to them: for this is the law and the prophets."*

Case Study: Thomas and Christina were a Christian couple who were both active in their local church before they met and throughout the entire time that they had courted before marrying. It was the first marriage for both but Thomas was several years older than Christina; still, the couple had the blessing of both sets of parents because they both had Christian testimonies.

Before Thomas officially proposed to Christina, the two had engaged in several serious conversations about what they both wanted in life and what their convictions were about how a Christian home should function. Seeing that they were on the same page about how they both felt about all of the big things – and realizing that he intended to pop the big question with a ring soon – Thomas asked Christina if there were any other questions that she wished to ask about him since they were clearly making plans to spend their lives together. She responded that she had no questions; but out

of a sense of responsibility to be completely honest with his future bride, Thomas confessed that he had previously had a physical relationship with someone else before they had met and that he had long since repented of the sin and asked God's forgiveness. He asked Christina if she still wished to make life plans together; and she replied in the affirmative, thanked him for being honest with her, and then assured him that she was still positive that she wished to spend her life with him.

Christina then asked Thomas if there was anything else that he wished to ask her; and he responded that he did have one concern that had been on his mind several times over the course of their courtship. She asked what it was; and he replied that he had a concern that she might be anorexic. He explained that he realized the fact that her being thin did not necessarily mean that she was anorexic; but he recalled several occasions where she had refused to eat a number of ordinary foods that everyone else was eating, and he also recalled her excusing herself to the restroom during or at the end of meals several times only to return with a look on her face as though she had just thrown up.

This was, understandably, a very difficult conversation for the two to have while they were discussing future wedding plans together; but given the fact that Thomas had just confessed his most embarrassing and private sin to her, he hoped that she did not feel that she was the only one being asked to reveal private things of a serious nature. Christina replied, though, that she definitely did not have anorexia nor any other eating disorder... that it was all in his imagination.

Still, the question was in Thomas' mind; so he broached the subject in private to Christina's parents on an occasion when it was just the three of them not long after his conversation with Christina about the matter. Both of her parents immediately dismissed the notion, even going so far as to make him feel ashamed for having asked the question. They easily dismissed the things that he brought up that might possibly suggest that it could be true; and they assured him that if it were true, they would know. Thomas dismissed his concern and soon presented an engagement ring to Christina.

The two were married in a beautiful church wedding with all of the attendant ceremony before driving away to begin their honeymoon together. Before the honeymoon had even ended, however, Thomas had discovered Christina purging in the bathroom of their hotel room on two occasions right after meals. On the first occasion, she dismissed it and said it had been "something that she ate." On the second occasion, she simply refused to discuss it. Also while still on the honeymoon, there were several other things that sent up red flags in Thomas' mind about Christina's behaviour. There were multiple times that she left entire portions of food on her plate at the various restaurants where they ate; and each time she declined to try the foods because she said that they looked as if the textures would not "stay down." These were not exotic foods but just ordinary dishes for most Americans according to Thomas. A couple of days into the honeymoon, Thomas jokingly asked Christina if she had forgotten her deodorant that morning because it was rather hot and humid; and there was a smell of body odor in the car as they traveled to their destination for the day. Christina responded that she actually never wore deodorant because she didn't want anything "on her skin." In case you're wondering how he could have missed this during their courtship, Thomas has since explained that the two were always very proper before marriage; and, other than holding hands, there really would have been few occasions where this could have possibly come to his attention.

The two returned from their honeymoon and began a routine in their new home together; but Christina's purging continued, almost on a daily basis immediately following the couple's supper each day, no matter whether they ate at home or ate out with other family members. Now being in close proximity to one another much of the time, Christina's aversion to wearing deodorant also began to become more of an issue for Thomas. In an effort to alleviate her husband's concern about the smell of body odor, Christina offered to try applying baby powder under her arms instead of using deodorant. Although it seemed odd to Thomas that one would be acceptable to his wife but not the other, he thanked her for offering to do it. Unfortunately, after a few short days, she decided to revert back to not using the talcum powder either. And once the two were living in the same house and using the same bathroom, there were other hygiene issues which arose. The hairbrush that Christina moved into their home together was completely matted with her long blonde hairs which had apparently collected in the bristles of the hairbrush for an extended period of time. When Thomas asked why she did not clean her hairbrush instead of leaving it lying on the bathroom counter like a furry ball, Christina replied that leaving the old hair on the brush instead of cleaning it helped with keeping down static in her hair when she brushed it. When he asked if there were some other possible solutions to the static problem, she simply shrugged and said, "That's the way that I like it." Apparently, though, the hairbrush – and even the lack of deodorant – was not the most difficult thing for Thomas as far as hygiene was concerned. He described the toilet in their bathroom as constantly having the smell of vomit and a constant residue of diarrhea due to his wife's eating habits.

After about a month of witnessing each of these things on a daily basis, Thomas sat his new wife down to have a frank discussion about her purging. After just a very few minutes, Christina acknowledged that she did, in fact, purge on a regular basis; but she argued that it was just "normal" for girls. At this point, Thomas expressed concern for his wife's health, citing not only the purging but also her apparent lack of healthy nutrition. He expressed his love for her and asked if she would consider seeing a doctor to at least discuss the matter. When Christina protested that their insurance probably wouldn't pay for it, her husband offered to pay for it out of pocket if necessary.

Christina called and scheduled an appointment with her doctor but said that she would only go if she could go alone. Reluctantly, Thomas agreed. The day for the appointment came; but Christina did not keep her appointment. Even more concerned now than originally, Thomas privately met with Christina's parents in an effort to get them to encourage her to go to the doctor to see if she needed some kind of help. Only then did her parents confess that they had taken Christina to her doctor in the past for the same concerns. Thomas asked why they had dismissed his concerns before the engagement when he had asked them about the very thing; and their response was simply that they had no "proof" that there was a problem. Apparently they had seen enough on their own to voice their concerns to her doctor before she graduated high school; but they had not considered that proof enough to have disclosed it to Thomas when he had asked before the engagement... and neither had Christina.

Still hoping to get Christina to at least see a doctor about the matter again, Thomas asked Christina if the two of them could sit down and talk with her parents about it privately; she protested but reluctantly agreed to the meeting. The meeting did not go well. Christina denied in front of her parents that she purged regularly after meals; and her parents suggested to Thomas that there must not be anything to be concerned about. Thomas was having trouble dealing with the fact that both Christina and her parents had withheld the information from him before their engagement about her earlier visit to the doctor over the issue – before he was even courting her – and also about the fact that now she had denied purging in front of her parents even after admitting it to him privately and after him witnessing it on numerous occasions for himself. In a last ditch effort to get Christina to reconsider at least seeing the doctor about it, Thomas asked someone at their church whom Christina trusted personally to speak to her privately about the purging; and she again denied that it ever happened.

For Thomas, who had grown up his entire life being taught to practice good hygiene and living in a home where his mother kept a clean house and taught her family to do likewise, the hygienic issues were on the verge of being more than he could handle some days just owing to the sights and smells in the small starter home; but it was the fraud and the continued lying that was the hardest for him to rectify in his mind and in his heart. He had been brought up to believe that divorce was wrong, and he had intentionally waited until he believed that he had found the right Christian girl to marry before proposing to anyone; but now he found himself in a mental and spiritual quandary.

Naive and still relatively young, Thomas made an appointment with a lawyer to ask if there was any way to have a marriage annulled. After listening to the young husband's story, the attorney replied that courts don't grant annulments any longer unless one or both of the spouses is under eighteen years of age. Thomas paid the attorney to file the necessary papers for divorce. Because he had not shared Christina's private matters, nor the attendant lies and fraud perpetrated by her and her parents about it before the marriage, with many people, there were a great many people who knew Thomas who expressed disappointment in him for having divorced his wife after living such a Godly life up to that point. Even his own family had trouble accepting the divorce because they, too, did not know of the private matters for some time.

This was not a situation that involved the question of virginity as the theoretical example in Deuteronomy, but it did involve lying about a serious matter before the marriage by both the bride and her parents. Furthermore, it included continued lying by the bride after the marriage. The hygienic issues in and of themselves did not constitute Biblical grounds for divorce in spite of how bad they may have been; and the husband's vow to be with his wife in sickness and in health certainly demanded that he see her through whatever mental, emotional, or spiritual issues were causing her problems; but the fraud about such a serious matter before the marriage covenant was made, especially when the question was specifically broached and lies were given by the bride and her parents, followed by continuing lies after the marriage, the husband found himself in a marriage where what he was made to believe he was getting was clearly not what he got. The original covenant was a fraud from the outset because of the lies; and his wife's continued lying to others about the matter after the marriage removed herself from under her husband's umbrella of covering. Perhaps the most ironic part of Thomas and Christina's story is that Thomas was the one who was not a virgin at the time of their marriage; but he had voluntarily disclosed it beforehand without even being asked as a

token of love and good faith. Christina did not provide the same transparency and good faith.

Lastly about the subject of fraud, I must reiterate that there is a difference if the spouse knows about such matters prior to marriage and still chooses to enter into the marriage covenant. At that point, he or she is entering into the contract with eyes wide open; and, for that reason, he or she will have no recourse for annulment or divorce after the fact because he or she was not misled; it was a willful decision to proceed based upon what they already knew to be the case. I will say, though, that many problems that later arise in marriages are directly related to things that were either lied about before the marriage or, more often than not, were intentionally left unsaid when they should have been disclosed. Most people in love are willing to overlook as much as their convictions will allow. BEFORE marriage. No one, however, likes finding themselves in a situation in which they feel as though they were misled in order to get them to arrive at a certain decision. That is fraud, and both man and God consider it a crime.

Biblical Ground #9: Abuse

It is an unfortunate reality that violence and abuse have been part of human existence since Cain killed Abel and that they will continue to be a part of human existence until God makes all things new at the end of this present world when the New Jerusalem descends from heaven to a new earth to begin eternity future for His own. Along with his other wicked devices, the Bible tells us that man was destroyed in Noah's flood because of his violence: *"The earth also was corrupt before God, and the earth was filled with violence. And God looked upon the earth, and, behold, it was corrupt; for all flesh had corrupted his way upon the earth. And God said unto Noah, The end of all flesh is come before me; for the earth is filled with violence through them; and, behold, I will destroy them with the earth"* (Genesis 6:11-13). Psalm 11:5 tells us exactly what God thinks about violence, *"The LORD trieth the righteous: but the wicked and him that loveth violence his soul hateth."* As regards His view of violence against innocents, He is not unclear either. Deuteronomy 21:9 says, "So shalt thou put away the *guilt of* innocent blood from among you, when thou shalt do *that which is* right in the sight of the LORD." And, again, in Exodus 23:7, *"Keep thee far from a false matter; and the innocent and righteous slay thou not: for I will not justify the wicked."* Scripture could not be more clear that God is opposed to violence against innocent souls.

It is clear from Scripture that God pleads the cause of the innocent against whom violence is committed. His vengeance against those who commit such acts is present in both this world and the next. But it is also clear in the Word of God that He does not expect man to sit back and allow these acts to take place without bringing them to an end, also. Indeed, God commands us to deliver the oppressed from the hands of the violent.

Jeremiah 22:3 commands, *"Thus saith the LORD; Execute ye judgment and righteousness, and deliver the spoiled out of the hand of the oppressor: and do no wrong, do no violence to the stranger, the fatherless, nor the widow, neither shed innocent blood in this place."* Society – and each of us individually – has the obligation to protect those who are innocent from abuse and violence. This does not mean that we as private citizens should take up some vigilante justice and begin taking the law into our own hands to enact whatever judgment we deem fit against the wicked: that is a responsibility reserved for the civil magistrates whom God has ordained to that purpose. It does mean, however, that we do exactly as the verse says and *"deliver the spoiled out of the hand of the oppressor."* While we are not authorized by either man's law or God to become judge, jury, and executioner against the wicked in our individual capacity, we are authorized – and commanded – to come to the rescue of innocents who are abused.

Everything that God expects of us is directly related to His attributes, to Who He is; and our God is a God of justice. A just God has no leniency with regard to the abuse of innocent souls. He simply will not countenance it. Human life is precious because man is created in the image of God; and whether it is the murder or any other abuse of an innocent person, an attack upon an innocent person is an affront to God and the marring of a person created in His image. Genesis 9:6 explains, *"Whoso sheddeth man's blood, by man shall his blood be shed: for in the image of God made he man."* This is generally understood as the moment when God ordained human government and gave some of His authority to mankind to execute justice. We know through both the Old and New Testaments that it is to the civil magistrates that He has given this authority. Nevertheless, we are all expected to deliver the spoiled out of the hand of the oppressor. You as an individual do not have the authority to execute someone for violence and abuse of an innocent soul, but you do have the authority – and the responsibility – to help deliver the innocent soul to safety... even if it is your own innocent soul that you are delivering.

Self-defense and self-preservation are also clearly taught in the Word of God. Not only are we obligated to defend other innocent souls that we see being abused, but we have just as great an obligation to defend our own selves from being abused by those who would do violence against us or our family members wrongfully. In the story of Esther, the Jewish people were encouraged to protect themselves against the violence initiated by Haman. In Nehemiah 4:17, of the Judahites who returned to rebuild the city and the wall of Jerusalem, it is recorded, *"They which builded on the wall, and they that bare burdens, with those that laded, every one with one of his hands wrought in the work, and with the other hand held a weapon."* In the New Testament, when Jesus was preparing his disciples for the persecution that was coming, we find this command, *"Then said he unto them, But now, he that hath a purse, let him take it, and likewise his scrip: and he that hath no sword, let him sell his garment, and buy one"* (Luke 22:36). The defense and preservation of ourselves and others is not only allowed Biblically; it is God's command.

Before we proceed, though, I must address an oft-misapplied passage of Scripture related to this topic. There are some who believe that Christians should take whatever abuse is meted out to them by others, even if it comes from the hand of a spouse and even if it becomes potentially life-threatening. They erroneously mischaracterize Jesus' teaching found in Matthew 5:38 and 39 which says, *"Ye have heard that it hath been said, An eye for an eye, and a tooth for a tooth:* **39***But I say unto you, That ye resist not evil: but whosoever shall smite thee on thy right cheek, turn to him the other also."* Not understanding the Old Testament context to which Jesus is referring nor the point that He is making, these people misconstrue Jesus' message to be something along the lines of, "Even if someone abuses you or commits violence against you, accept it and go on." This completely unBiblical interpretation of this passage has resulted in countless numbers of women and children (and even some men) suffering prolonged abuse at the hand of spouses and parents over the years. This horribly wrong interpretation of what Jesus is saying has not only caused innocent people to accept their abuse but has also caused them to remain in the abusive situation... both of which fly in the face of what we already have seen to be true of the nature of our God and His commands for us to defend and preserve ourselves since we are created in His image. The point which Jesus is making in this passage – and the ONLY point that He is making in this passage – is that, as believers, we should not practice retaliation against those who wrong us but, rather, leave vengeance to God Who is a much better Judge and executioner of such things. This is the reason that Jesus specifically quoted the Old Testament references to "an eye for an eye" type of retaliation which was part of the Mosaic Law that we find recorded in Exodus 21:24 and Leviticus 24:20. He was teaching in this instance that as Christians we should not strike back when we are wronged but pray for those who do wrong and allow God to execute justice on our behalf. Furthermore, He intentionally spoke of someone smiting us on the cheek – a slap, in other words. No one should be slapped in the face, even when it is a child being disciplined by his parent; but the fact remains that a slap on the cheek is not generally a life-threatening situation in and of itself. Even if we turn the other cheek and are slapped on the second cheek, two slaps to the face do not generally pose a life-threatening situation which require us to strike out in order to defend our lives. Jesus did not teach, though, that we must endure any kind of life-threatening or serious abuse; nor did He teach that we should remain in the situation or return to the very situation where we were previously abused. Christians, especially pastors, should be extremely cautious about counseling others to remain in any situation in which they are genuinely being abused. The Bible clearly does not teach this.

So what constitutes abuse? If you read a dozen different sources, you are likely to get a dozen different answers to that question. Some answers are better than others, but I found a difficult time finding one that seemed to adequately cover all of the bases without overshooting and delving into potentially normal situations. So here's my own short answer to the question: abuse is any act or threat of act which causes unjustified pain. I think it is important that we include the threat of an act which causes pain because, ultimately, even the threat, itself, is a form of abuse. Because of the day in which we live, it's also important to include the caveat that it is "unjustified" pain; this is necessary because some influences in the world would lump even loving, Biblical discipline with abuse. With this definition in mind, then, it necessarily means that abuse may include more than mere physical violence; for pain often comes in other forms including psychological, emotional, and spiritual. Usually abuse involves more than one form; but even one of these is enough to constitute abuse.

Physical abuse is the form which probably first comes to mind when abuse is mentioned and oftentimes is the easiest to recognize because it frequently is accompanied by physical marks and bruises which can be seen with the eye. The Bible passages that we have already seen in this chapter plainly teach that violence against innocents is not only a sin but, in the eyes of God, a wickedness that He takes personal, as well. All believers are commanded to deliver the abused from their oppressors; and this includes delivering one's self if it be the case.

In the past, there has been a hesitancy on the part of many, even among Christians, to acknowledge psychological and emotional abuse. Fortunately, today there is less skepticism over these forms of abuse than in the past. Psychological and emotional abuse can be accomplished by the perpetrator in a number of ways, but it almost invariably includes some amount of belittling – intentionally trying to make the abused feel unimportant, stupid, or worthless. Sometimes the abuser may come right out and say those things aloud; but other times it may be implied in comments repeatedly without being spoken outright. The one thing that is almost universally true of this type of abuse is that it is generally prolonged; That is, it usually occurs over an extended amount of time. In this sense, it is not the same kind of abuse as an immediate, physical attack which can be life-threatening due to physical trauma; but it is the constant drip, drip, drip like the Chinese water torture which little-by-little erodes the victims' view of themselves and can, in some instances, be just as life-threatening.

Case Study: Hank and Abigail had been married for nearly ten years. Somewhere around year two of the marriage, the two decided to begin trying to have a baby. For three years the couple tried earnestly, with Abigail even going to the point of studying her times of the month and taking body temperatures in an effort to find the scientifically best times to try to become pregnant. After three years of trying, however, the couple was frustrated and decided that they should each see a doctor to determine if there was a physical reason that they had not yet been able to conceive. After seeing their respective doctors, it was determined that while he was not technically sterile, Hank had a low sperm count that would make it much less likely that the couple would ever get pregnant.

Both of the couple were emotionally crushed by the realization that they might not ever be able to have children naturally. Hank felt that he was somehow insufficient, even though it was owing to no fault of his own; and Abigail was just sad about it in general. The two discussed some

different artificial solutions, but none were really affordable to the couple. They also discussed adoption, but neither was certain that they wanted to do that, either.

For a short time, both Hank and Abigail were sad together but tried to encourage each other; but as time went on, Abigail became increasingly unhappy about the situation. The day came when, in the heat of an argument about something totally unrelated, she accused Hank of being less than a man because he couldn't even give her a child. The words were not even out of her mouth before she realized what she had done. The moment was so traumatic for them both that the argument abruptly ended, and neither said another word about it. Though she felt bad for having said it at first, the next time that Abigail became angry with Hank about something else, the words slipped out again. And then again. Eventually, Abigail became increasingly disinterested in having marital relations; but it was the fact that she became comfortable over time with making cutting remarks about his manhood or about comparing him to other men, even men that they knew, that took its toll on both Hank and their marriage in general.

There was never any physical abuse of any kind between the two spouses; but after nearly five years of enduring Abigail's constant reminders that he was "less than a man," Hank filed for divorce. Abigail never struck her husband physically, but the constant mental and emotional abuse wore on him over time. She failed to love her husband as herself; she failed to be submissive and show honour to her husband; and she abused him. I have intentionally included this example because few of us think of wives as abusers, but abuse is abuse no matter at whose hands, even when it is mental or emotional abuse. It is disrespectful to both the other individual... and to God.

For Christians, there is also such a thing as spiritual abuse. While the Apostle Paul makes it clear in I Corinthians that believers who find themselves already married to unbelievers should remain married if the unbeliever is content to remain, it does not mean that a believer should be forced by another to violate Biblical commands. This may arise in the form of being coerced into doing things that we should not or in the form of being coerced into not doing things that we are commanded by God to do. For example, a wife who is prohibited by her husband from attending a Bible-believing church or from reading her Bible finds herself in a very similar situation to the prophet Daniel in the Old Testament when he was commanded by the civil law to not pray to God for thirty days. His response was to continue to pray because God commands it of believers. Daniel 6:10 tells us, *"Now when Daniel knew that the writing was signed, he went into his house; and his windows being open in his chamber toward Jerusalem, he kneeled upon his knees three times a day, and prayed, and gave thanks before his God, as he did aforetime."* Notice that he did not begin praying after the law was passed; it was already his practice of doing so. Daniel did not contravene the law because he was trying to protest in some way; he was merely being faithful to God as he had always done. The same would be true of a wife who was told that she could not read her Bible nor attend a Bible-believing church. By the same token, a husband or wife who is subjected by their spouse to participation in worship that is idolatrous would also be another example of spiritual abuse. Some husbands – and even wives – have sought to coerce their spouses into attending cults or churches which teach things contrary to Scripture; and some have even forced their spouses to associate with such blatant forms of idolatry as seances, oija boards, witchcraft, and the occult. These examples are not dissimilar from the situation which faced the three Hebrew children who were thrown into the burning, fiery furnace for their refusal to bow down to the image erected by King Nebuchadnezzar. Their response, as recorded in Daniel 3, was very bold: *"Shadrach, Meshach, and Abednego, answered and said to the king, O Nebuchadnezzar, we are not careful to answer thee in this matter. If it be so, our God whom we serve is able to deliver us from the burning fiery furnace, and he will deliver us out of thine hand, O king. But if not, be it known unto thee, O king, that we will not serve thy gods, nor worship the golden image which thou hast set up."* There is also the instance recorded in the Book of Ezra where the men of Judah had sinned by intermarrying with the Canaanite women around them despite God's clear command not to do so. Though it is not explicitly stated in the passage, it is implied that their pagan wives were still practicing pagan worship to Ba'al and Ashtoreth even while living in their homes with Jewish husbands. Ezra 10:10-12 records what God commanded in that situation: *"And Ezra the priest stood up, and said unto them, Ye have transgressed, and have taken strange wives, to increase the trespass of Israel. Now therefore make confession unto the LORD God of your fathers, and do his pleasure: and separate yourselves from the people of the land, and from the strange wives. Then all the congregation answered and said with a loud voice, As thou hast said, so must we do."* The men then met, one by one, with the judges and were divorced from their idolatrous wives. When it comes to situations in which believers find themselves already married to unbelievers (or believers who act like unbelievers), the default position should always be to follow the instructions recorded in I Corinthians where Paul said to remain with the unbelieving spouse if the unbelieving spouse is willing to do so. This presupposes, though, that the unbelieving spouse allows the believer to worship God freely, without abuse for doing so or coercion to do otherwise. It is doubtful, however, that this applies to situations in which a believer is required to disobey clear Biblical commands and violate sacred conscience by remaining.

It seems likely, if not definitely, that a spouse who is being abused will also have Biblical grounds for divorce based upon other grounds that we have already discussed (i.e., not loving spouse as self, treating a wife as a slave, etc.); but we are treating it separately here because it provides Biblical grounds for divorce in and of itself. In addition to the passages of Scripture that we have seen which deal with physical abuse, there are numerous other passages that deal with emotional and psychological abuse. Proverbs 18:21 says, *"Death and life are in the power of the tongue."* And Proverbs 15:4 says, *"A wholesome tongue is a tree of life: but perverseness therein is a breach in the spirit."* James 3:8 tells us, *"But the tongue can no man tame; it is an unruly evil, full of deadly poison."* Proverbs 4:14 says, *"Enter not into the path of the wicked, and go not in the way of evil men."* And Proverbs 14:16 instructs, *"A wise man feareth, and departeth from evil."* There is a reason that God commands us to avoid evil and violent people.

Many spouses, especially wives, have convinced themselves that they should remain in an abusive marriage because they view it as an act of loyalty to God because of the sanctity of marriage. They view themselves as sacrificially portraying an obedient believer and a submissive servant of God by staying and enduring the abuse. Their desire is surely to demonstrate to others, perhaps even their own children, how sacred and permanent God intends marriage to be. I have even had husbands and wives both over the years tell me in counseling that their own parents have given them this advice. I submit to you, though, that this is not only incorrect; but remaining in such an abusive marriage can actually rise to the level of sin on the part of the spouse that chooses to remain while being abused. Since it is true that marriage is intended to picture to the world the relationship between Christ and His church, in order for that to be an accurate picture, the relationship must be a wholesome, loving relationship. A marriage which involves abuse of one spouse by the other is actually projecting to everyone around it a very false picture of the relationship of a loving God to His bride, the church. So, then, wives and husbands who remain in an abusive marriage are not doing themselves, their neighbors, their children, or God any favours; in fact, they may be giving their own children or others assumptions about marriage which may lead to disastrous consequences for them later in life.

Throughout many years of counseling, both as a pastor and as a layman, one thing which I have witnessed in almost every case of abuse is an effort by the abuser to isolate the victim from anyone who may be a potential support system and means of escape. It is important that anyone who is being abused becomes conscious of this possibility because it often happens before the abused even realizes that it is happening; and, unfortunately, it sometimes is not realized until bridges have been burned and ties have been cut that could have offered help. It is not unusual for abusers to systematically isolate their victims from friends, family, coworkers, church family, and others; and it is typically done in a different manner with different members of the potential support system so that the victim is not cognizant of the overarching plan to do so.

Abuse, whether it is emotional, psychological, spiritual, or physical, is a violation of the fundamental basis of the marriage covenant and is Biblical grounds for divorce.

Biblical Ground #10: Dealing Treacherously

Malachi 2:14-16 says, *"Yet ye say, Wherefore? Because the LORD hath been witness between thee and the wife of thy youth, against whom thou hast dealt treacherously: yet is she thy companion, and the wife of thy covenant. And did not he make one? Yet had he the residue of the spirit. And wherefore one? That he might seek a godly seed. Therefore take heed to your spirit, and let none deal treacherously against the wife of his youth. For the LORD, the God of Israel, saith that he hateth putting away: for one covereth violence with his garment, saith the LORD of hosts: therefore take heed to your spirit, that ye deal not treacherously."* The message in this passage is that Jehovah had stopped accepting the offerings of many in Israel because they had committed the sin of "dealing treacherously" with the wives of their youth. In other words, they had tired of the wives who had given themselves to their husbands in marriage while they were young; and now the husbands treated them as less than wives and, in too many cases, had simply thrown them away in divorce when they no longer "had any delight in them" as we have seen previously.

God viewed (and views) it as treacherous when a husband and wife marry and then, after years of married life together, one or the other grows tired of the other and is ready to either "move on to greener pastures" or simply be free and single again. He calls it "treacherous" because the spouse who has violated the marriage covenant in treating his or her spouse as less than should be treated has stolen the good years of the spouse's youth away and then sought to throw them away like throwing out the trash at the end of the day. Some would argue that this is just the same Biblical grounds for divorce as we have already dealt with under the category of treating a spouse as a slave, or as less than a marriage partner. However, I have listed it as a separate Biblical ground for divorce here in our study because, logically speaking, it is (or can be) a different offense. Every spouse who "deals" treacherously has necessarily begun treating his or her spouse as less than a marriage partner; but not all of those who treat their spouses as slaves have been married long enough that it could reasonably be described as "dealing treacherously" with the wife (or husband) of their youth.

In this passage of the Bible, we see just how sickened God is by this abandoning of a marriage partner who has given years of service, love, and commitment to his or her spouse. He is so incensed by it, in fact, that He refuses to accept their gifts and sacrifices, which is a serious matter since that was the way that He had specifically told the children of Israel that they were to approach Him. The verse just before the passage that we have quoted in Malachi explains this: *"And this have ye done again, covering the altar of the LORD with tears, with weeping, and with crying out, insomuch that he regardeth not the offering any more, or receiveth it with good will at your hand."* It is a serious thing to have broken fellowship with God; but it is a much more grave matter when the fellowship is broken and He will not allow one to approach Him; for there is no remedy for the broken fellowship with Him if we cannot even approach with our gifts and sacrifices in a show of repentance. This does not mean that the sin resulted in a loss of personal salvation, but it means that anyone who was committing this sin had no access to God until they ceased committing it.

Some have erroneously taken the phrase in verse 16 which reads, *"For the LORD, the God of Israel, saith that he hateth putting away"* to mean that He does not approve of divorce because He hates it; for the phrase *"putting away"* is a direct reference to divorce. This is not what the passage is teaching, however. As we have already previously seen in this book, God, Himself, put away Israel with a writ of divorce; so He is not opposed to divorce, itself. Rather, He is opposed to the *need* for divorce... because the behaviour that results in the need for divorce should not happen in the first place. He chastises the men of Israel in Malachi for dealing treacherously with their wives. He does not, however, chastise wives for wishing for divorces from sorry husbands who have dealt treacherously with them. Rather, Jehovah is sympathetic to wives who have been treated thusly. We can only assume that He is also sympathetic to husbands who are treated thusly, as well.

Case Study: Jeremy and Allison got married when they were both in their early twenties. They had an average life in an average neighborhood with average incomes. Along the way, the couple had two boys who were involved in sports and did well in school. The couple never had any major problems in their marriage, only the occasional disagreements as do all couples.

When their oldest son graduated high school, though, Jeremy seemed to begin going through what pop psychologists refer to as a "mid-life crisis." The fact is that all husbands and wives must work hard all of the time to make sure that their marriages do not grow stale; but Jeremy convinced himself that his unmarried coworkers had "the good life" - no responsibilities and no commitments to just one woman. Because Jeremy worked for a Christian man who attended their church, though, he knew that if he divorced Allison so that he could go "sow his wild oats," his boss was likely to look for a reason to fire him; so instead of divorcing her, he decided to just ignore her and begin allowing himself the liberty of living just a little bit like he was single even though he was still married. He still paid the bills and kept up the facade in front of everyone else that they knew, but privately he was disrespectful to Allison and spent most of his time ogling other women. He even made such a habit of speaking in a condescending manner to his wife that their two boys began to do the same.

This sad story is a perfect example of the Bible's prohibition against husbands dealing treacherously with their wives. This husband treated his wife much differently after years of marriage than he had treated her when they were first married or when he had been courting her. As a faithful wife of many years, even though she was older and arguably less physically attractive than when she was in her twenties, she was entitled to still be loved and honoured and treated well by the husband to whom she had given the best years of her life. For him to treat her differently after he had received years of loving faithfulness from her was a dishonour to his wife and to the God of the marriage covenant.

While husbands (or wives) who have dealt treacherously with their wives (or husbands) should not divorce their spouses, it is because they should not be treating their spouses treacherously, not because their spouses are not entitled to bills of divorcement. For those who deal treacherously with a spouse have begun to deal with their marriage partner as less than a husband or wife... and this is a breach of the marriage covenant.

Biblical Grounds: Summary

We have examined ten different Biblical grounds for marriage that are outlined in Scripture. All of them are rooted in violations of the marriage covenant that God created for the first marriage; and all are violations of the marriage vows that each husband and wife who have ever married have made to one another, whether they were audibly spoken or not. The choice to enter into the institution of marriage which was created by God necessarily means that each husband and wife have assented to His rules for marriage, even in those cases where they have not explicitly said so... and even in those situations in which they claim to not even believe in His existence. He is the Authority Who created marriage, and everyone who participates in it is subject to His rules for the institution. As such, He is the Authority to whom we must look to oversee and protect the institution. He has chosen to protect this sacred institution by proscribing its rules and by delineating the situations which cause it to be breached; and in those situations in which it is breached, He allows – and in some instances *commands* – divorce... not for the purpose of destroying the sanctity of marriage but for the purpose of preserving its sanctity.

PART 5

I Have Biblical Grounds for Divorce. Now What?

Coming to the realization that you have Biblical grounds for divorce in your marriage is likely both a breath of hope to you but also still a cause for sadness. Divorce has been, I think rightly, compared to a death in the family. When we begin marriage as husband or wife, no one anticipates (or I hope no one anticipates) it ending in divorce. We invest ourselves into our marriages, hopefully all of ourselves into it; and if it fails and ends in divorce, we all have a tendency as humans to view ourselves as failures to some degree – even if it was the other party who brought about the grounds for divorce. Perhaps more than the feeling of failure, though, is the sadness at realizing that we have poured so much of our heart, soul, time, and love into a relationship which is now perhaps coming to an end. For a believer, it is never a time for rejoicing and can even be hard despite the other party having created Biblical grounds for the divorce.

In spite of whatever feelings of despondency may plague your mind and heart at realizing that you do, in fact, have Biblical grounds to end your marriage, there is certainly still room for hope... both for yourself, your spouse, your children, your extended family, and for everyone else who will potentially be touched by the divorce.

Divorce or Reconciliation

The first question that you must ask yourself once you have established that you do, in fact, have Biblical grounds for divorce is this... do you wish to pursue divorce or do you wish to pursue reconciliation? The reality is that most pastors and other divorce counselors seem predisposed to encourage everyone that they counsel either one direction or the other. Some, especially secular counselors, almost exclusively counsel in favour of divorce and starting over new with someone else. Then there are some, including many pastors, who almost exclusively counsel that even if you have Biblical grounds for divorce, you should seek reconciliation. Both Scripturally and legally, once the marriage covenant is breached, the marriage covenant ceases to exist in God's eyes and generally in the law's eyes. Or perhaps we should say, the obligations to the marriage covenant cease to exist. It then becomes the decision of the spouse who has been wronged to determine whether he or she wishes to pursue a path of divorce or reconciliation. I sincerely believe that a Christian may choose either path with a clear conscience once it is established that Biblical grounds for divorce exist. Let's be honest, they either exist or they do not exist. If they exist, then the other party has broken the covenant, in which case you are free from your own obligations to the covenant and are at liberty to pursue finding a spouse who wishes to be faithful to the marriage covenant so that you might enjoy married life the way that God has generally planned for all men and women... and you should feel the liberty to do that without feeling guilty for it. On the other hand, you have invested much of yourself in the relationship; and it could turn out to be that your marriage might not only be salvageable but, perhaps, ultimately end up being the kind of marriage that it should have been all along.

So how do you begin to make such a monumental decision? I think that it all hinges on the damage that has been done already and the sincere sorrow (if any) on the part of the offending spouse. We must remember that divorce is allowed by God for two specific reasons: 1) it is for the protection of the innocent against those who would do them wrong and then seek to keep them imprisoned in a life of less than what God intends for each of us, and 2) it is for the protection of His own good name and testimony since marriage is supposed to provide everyone around us with a picture of His relationship with His church. Perhaps a good question to ask yourself if you're already at this point in your own marriage is whether you feel better about walking away from the marriage or better about trying to restore it. The truth is that only you – with God's help – can answer this question.

Because you have reached this point due to the fact that your spouse has given you Biblical grounds for divorce (otherwise, hopefully you are not still genuinely contemplating it), you must assess whether your spouse is willing to take the steps necessary to remedy whatever provided you the Biblical grounds in the first place. If he or she is not falling all over themselves to correct whatever needs to be corrected, as a pastor I would probably counsel you to accept the right of divorce that God has extended to you and begin to take the necessary steps toward that end. For it would only be appropriate for you to even consider trying to reconcile the marriage if your spouse is willing to correct the things that need to be corrected; otherwise, the marriage will still not be a right picture of Christ and the church, and He will still not be able to bless the marriage. Furthermore, continuing in a wrong relationship, as we have already established, simply does damage to the testimony of the Lord's love and also to the testimony of what a wholesome marriage is supposed to be. Continuing to pursue reconciliation when the other party has said, either with their words or with their actions, that they have no intention of changing the things which are wrong in the marriage would not only likely doom the marriage a second time but could be giving your children, your grandchildren, your nieces and nephews, your coworkers, and others a wrong view of marriage that will end up causing them heartache in their own lives later, as well.

If the other party does seem genuinely repentant and willing to change, the next question becomes whether or not too much damage has already been done for them to have a reasonable chance at reestablishing the trust that their actions have destroyed. Undoubtedly, no matter which Biblical grounds you have for ending your marriage, the problems did not begin overnight and have probably been brewing for some time. As we have seen, some of the Biblical grounds for ending a marriage may take weeks, months, or even years to rise to the level of legitimate grounds for divorce; and with the notable exceptions of adultery and abuse, all of them should be examined in view of the "light and transient" test that we've already discussed. With all of this having been said, it is likely that whatever the grounds for divorce, trust, in some form or fashion, has probably been reduced systematically over time. In order for there to be a genuine chance of success at reconciliation, the offended party must be willing to forgive the offender and must also be willing to allow the necessary amount of time for the offender to rebuild the trust that has been eroded; and this, in most cases, is not something which can happen right away. Are you willing to give your spouse the time necessary to rebuild the trust that has been eroded, or is it at the point that no matter how hard he or she may try, it is unlikely that he or she will ever again be able to regain the trust that was lost? If you adjudge that it is impossible or even improbably that your spouse can regain the trust that they have lost, you should exercise your right of divorce. To do otherwise would place you in the position of imprisoning someone who is hoping for reconciliation when you know in your own heart that it is no longer a possibility. If you have reached this place, you must remember that it is not your fault that you are at this place; and it is not your fault that Biblical grounds exist. There is no sin nor disgrace (and, therefore, there should be no guilt) in exercising your right of divorce if proper Biblical grounds for it have been created by the other party.

What does genuine repentance look like? The Bible gives us a very precise picture of what genuine repentance looks like; and while it is given in the context of our relationship as believers with our Heavenly Father, it is no different in our relationships with each other. I John 1:9 says, "If we confess our sins, he is faithful and just to forgive us *our* sins, and to cleanse us from all unrighteousness." The passage says that if we want to be forgiven, we must "confess" our sins. So what does it mean to "confess" our sins? Well, the average person would say that it means to give a list of the wrongs that we've done; but that definition comes up short of the Biblical definition of "confess." The Greek word in this verse which is translated "confess" is "homologeo" which is a verb that literally means "to say the same thing." This means that God's definition of confession is much more than just listing our sins; it is saying the same things about our sin that He says about our sin. When we agree with God about the ugliness, dirtiness, awfulness of our sins, only *then* are we actually confessing them. Then there is the act of actually naming our sins. Too often, we allow our children – and even adults – to escape true confession by letting them get by with such "confessions" as "I'm sorry I did wrong." They may be genuinely sorrowful for doing wrong, but it is not confession unless they have named what it was that they did wrong AND agreed with you about how wrong it was. This is confession. So in returning to our subject of divorce, you must answer for yourself whether your spouse has actually "confessed" his or her sins that created the breach of the marriage covenant. Were the specific wrongs admitted? If not, they are not likely to be corrected. Did your spouse agree with you (and, more importantly, with God) about how wrong his or her actions were? If not, there is not genuine repentance.

Forgiveness and Staying

Do I have to forgive my spouse and does it mean that I have to stay if I forgive? These are two very important questions that I have been asked often as pastor. The answers are important not only for your spouse but also for your own spiritual health and well-being. The answer to the forgiveness question hinges upon the sincerity of the one who is wanting forgiveness. In order to determine whether you should grant forgiveness, we must again return to the passage of Scripture that we just saw in I John 1:9. Even though the verse deals with God forgiving us, it is just as applicable to us forgiving others; for we as Christians are supposed to reflect Him in all aspects of our own lives, including our decisions about forgiveness. Many of us were taught – wrongly, I might add – since we were children that we are to forgive anyone who has wronged us. We hear that today from schools, children's books, Oprah, the curly-headed preacher from Texas on television, and more than a few other preachers, as well. But is it right? More importantly, is it Biblical? The answer is "no," it isn't. Go back and read I John 1:9 again. Does it say that God automatically forgives everyone who does wrong against Him? Of course not. It says that *"IF we confess our sins, he is faithful and just to forgive us."* That little word "if" is actually a really big word when it comes to its importance in this verse. The verse literally tells us that God only forgives us when we confess our sins; and we've already seen what it means to actually "confess" our sins. So, then, the world's philosophy that you should automatically forgive anyone who wrongs you is completely unScriptural. Granting forgiveness to someone who has not genuinely confessed and repented of their sin is not only unBiblical; but it teaches everyone watching something false about how God deals with us... which means that they are less likely to do what God expects the next time that they are wanting forgiveness from Him, also. Unless your spouse has genuinely confessed the things that he or she has done wrong, enumerating them and agreeing about their awfulness in sincerity, you should not grant forgiveness. Does this mean that you should allow bitterness over it to eat you up from the inside because they did not confess and repent in earnest? No, of course not; you should simply accept that the matter is now between them and God unless they come back to you at a later time and confess the right way when they ask your forgiveness. On the other hand, if they do confess their wrongs against you Biblically and with sincerity (as much as you can ascertain), you are commanded to forgive them. This is important for them to begin the process of getting their lives right with God and man. The need to feel forgiven is perhaps the greatest need that mankind has. It is also important for you to accurately reflect God by learning to forgive when the proper conditions are met.

Please read this next part very carefully: Just because you are obligated to forgive the offending spouse does NOT mean that you must take them back and does not mean that you must remain married if the covenant has been breached and you have Biblical grounds for divorce. Again, people oftentimes incorrectly accept the world's philosophy that if you forgive someone who has wronged you then you must forget what they did and act as though it never happened. This is neither wise nor is it Biblical. Just because you are obligated to forgive someone, even multiple times, if he or she is sincere each time they confess their wrong and ask forgiveness, it does not mean that you must put yourself in a position to be wronged by them again. God forgives us each time that we genuinely exercise I John 1:9 in our lives as Christians; but He does not forget that we have done the same thing in the past. Yes, I realize that the Bible talks about God not remembering the sins of Israel... or of his bride, the church; but those passages are in reference to Him not remembering our iniquities in eternity future, after the new heavens and the new earth and the new Jerusalem have been set up for forever. This is exactly the context in both Hebrews 10:14-17 and again in Hebrews 8:12, as well as every other similar passage in both the Old and New Testaments. For proof from the Scriptures that He still remembers what we did the last time that we sinned and did the same old thing again, we need only recall His relationship with Israel over and over again throughout the entire Old Testament. We read of Him forgiving Israel repeatedly, but we also read that He finally reached a point with both Israel and Judah at which He allowed them to go into captivity because of their repeated adultery (idolatry with other gods). This proves that even though He forgave them repeatedly, He did not forget their previous offenses. To do so would mean that He would have to allow them to make a fool of Him. And for you to act as though your spouse has not wronged you or abused you or committed adultery against you, thereby giving them occasion to do the same thing again as though you were oblivious to their past indiscretions, would make you a fool as well... literally speaking, of course. No, God does not expect you to forget the wrongs done even if you grant forgiveness. If you make the choice to allow the possibility of reconciliation, you should do that with full awareness of what the offending spouse has done in the past and tread with caution as you move forward until that trust has been earned again. But if you should choose to exercise the right of divorce because you have Biblical grounds, you are also free to do that even while granting forgiveness; granting forgiveness does not mean that you must remain in the marriage.

If I have Biblical grounds for divorce but choose to allow the possibility for reconciliation with my spouse, do I have to remain physically present in the same home while doing so? There certainly is no obligation for a spouse who has Biblical grounds for divorce to remain in the same home with the offending spouse, even if the decision has been made to try to reconcile the marriage. It could be important to live separately for a time, particularly if the cause of the grounds for divorce had something to do with drugs, alcohol, or abuse. In this instance, physically remaining in the home could potentially subject the victim to even more victimization. If a period of time is needed for the offending spouse to "get clean" or simply to demonstrate that a spiritual change has taken place, there is no prohibition against a voluntary separation for a time while both spouses are trying to work things out. What would not be okay, however, would be for the two spouses to live separately while still legally married and begin acting as though they are unmarried, seeing other people. Although this is precisely what the world generally calls a "separation" in a marriage – and what the world expects to be the case – it is not acceptable for Christians who are still married to act as though they are unmarried. Christians who have Biblical grounds for divorce must make a clear, clean cut decision... either to remain in the marriage, at least for the time being, and work towards reconciliation... or pursue a divorce decree. There is no wiggle room as far as God is concerned for married believers to begin seeing other people while they "work things out" with their spouses. A physical separation is completely understandable, and perhaps even necessary; but having extra-marital affairs while doing it is neither understandable nor acceptable.

The Right Process for Ending Your Marriage

If I have Biblical grounds for divorce and choose to terminate the marriage, what is the right process to do so? Hopefully, except in the case of an immediate breach of the marriage covenant as with adultery or abuse, you have presented your spouse with a list of grievances and given opportunity for true repentance and for the grievances to be corrected. If, however, over time they have not been corrected and you have reached the point that you clearly have Biblical grounds for divorce and that is the course of action that you have determined for yourself, there are some very important things that you should do to properly exit the marriage without, yourself, falling into a pitfall of sin in the process. It is important to do things the right way, even when exiting a marriage, lest your testimony be harmed even though you were the party which had Biblical grounds for divorce. After making the final decision to dissolve your marriage, you must make it clear to your spouse that he or she has created a breach in the marriage covenant and, in so doing, has already terminated the marriage, at least in God's eyes. Some of the things which you should do to make this clear include: stating this clearly to your spouse, although this does not have to be done in person if there is any fear of reprisal; removing your wedding ring, the outward symbol of the covenant which no longer exists, since continuing to wear it would constitute a false statement; ceasing all intimate relations with your spouse since that is something reserved exclusively for married partners; and beginning the legal process to receive a writ of divorcement, although it does not necessarily have to be initiated by the offended party, as we shall see from Scripture shortly.

What are the obligations of the spouse who has committed the acts which constitute Biblical grounds for divorce? As odd as it might sound, there is good reason to include in this book a brief discussion of the things that the offending spouse should do if he or she finds himself in a situation where the end of the marriage is in sight. I say this because everyone has made mistakes before, and this includes even some of the best Christians who have ever lived. Even King David, a man after God's own heart, committed sins that few of us have ever even contemplated; so there is the possibility that someone reading this book might just be the person sitting in the guilty seat rather than the victim seat in the tragic ending to a marriage. It is important to remember that God is constantly seeking to work in our lives if we belong to Him and are His children. This includes the moments when things are going well and also the moments when things seem bleakest. Sometimes – in fact, oftentimes – those moments are a result of our own failures and sins. But even during these times, it is important to remember that God is still working to make and mold us into what He wants us to be. Just like with Gideon in the Bible, God sees us not for who we are today but who we could be if we lived by faith. So, if you should find yourself in the situation of realizing that your marriage is coming to an end... and it's your fault... realize that you can be forgiven and that God still has a perfect will for your life from this day forward. Regarding your spouse's decision to pursue a divorce, here are the obligations that the guilty spouse has in this situation: 1) Seek to understand what you did wrong; and for those things where you've genuinely done wrong, repent, confess them to God and your spouse, and cease doing them. 2) Ask your spouse for an opportunity at reconciliation only if you are genuinely willing to acknowledge your sins and to forsake them. 3) Realize that even if you are sincere, it may not be enough at this point if you have already given your spouse Biblical grounds for divorce. If this is the case, everything is not lost no matter how bleak the future seems right now. As tragic as it is anytime that a marriage ends, if this becomes the catalyst in your life for you to become the man or woman that God wants you to be, this doesn't have to be the way that your story ends. Even God's chastening in our lives is a gift of love and grace because He wants us to become the believer that we should be. 4) If you owe your spouse a divorce, as the Bible says in multiple instances, because you have broken your marriage covenant in one of the ways that we've outlined in this book, follow God's command and grant your spouse a writ of divorce if they wish it. There is nothing honourable about choosing to "fight for your marriage" by refusing to grant your spouse a divorce that is deserved after you have broken the covenant. 5) Seek God's will for your life from this point on and pursue it with everything that you possess within you.

When is it Officially Over?

When is the marriage covenant technically ended? There are two answers to this question, and both are correct. In the eyes of the Lord – the One Who created the institution of marriage – the marriage covenant ceases to exist the moment that 1) there is a breach of the covenant with one or more of the Biblical grounds that we've already examined and 2) the aggrieved spouse has followed the steps outlined above in this part of the book, putting the offending spouse on notice that the marriage is permanently terminated and following through with those other steps to cease all marital relations. In the eyes of others – and particularly the government of the state in which you live – the covenant is not technically ended until a judge acknowledges it by granting a writ of divorce. Deuteronomy 24:1 and 2 states, *"When a man hath taken a wife, and married her, and it come to pass that she find no favour in his eyes, because he hath found some uncleanness in her: then let him write her a bill of divorcement, and give it in her hand, and send her out of his house. And when she is departed out of his house, she may go and be another man's wife."* Among other things, this passage explains the importance of having the "bill of divorcement" or the "writ of divorce," or, in other words, "the actual piece of paper that says you're divorced." The purpose of obtaining the legal document is so that both spouses may move on and are free to marry other spouses. The piece of paper is not necessary in order for God to see that the covenant has been broken and that the victim is free to remarry; it is necessary so that *others* may know that it is ok for the person to move on and marry someone else. Without the legal document, it would simply look to others as though the spouse who was the actual victim and had actual Biblical grounds for divorce was being immoral, which, in Bible times, also meant stoning for adultery. Even today when we have done away with stoning people for adultery in our part of the world, it is still necessary for testimony's sake that everyone else know that the marriage covenant has been ended prior to them seeing one of the spouses, even the victim, with someone else romantically. So, then, the offended spouse who had Biblical grounds for divorce may be free in the sight of God to enter into a romantic relationship with someone else as soon as they have made the announcement to their guilty spouse and ceased all marital relations; but that spouse should not commence with a romantic relationship in front of others until the writ of divorce is had in hand for testimony's sake.

As we come to the conclusion of this book, I wish to reiterate the point that with which I began, namely that my desire is that this book might *prevent* divorce rather than encourage it. All husbands and wives would do well to have a more thorough understanding of the marriage covenant and the obligations under it than most people have today. Marriage is taken too lightly by society today; and, consequently, so, too, is divorce; it is the reason that divorce rates continue to climb while the percentage of romantic couples choosing to even begin a marriage is declining. Only with a truly Biblical understanding and appreciation for the marriage covenant and its attending obligations to one another can a husband and wife hope to enjoy a lifetime of marital bliss as God intends. I sincerely hope that a deeper understanding of that covenant and commitment by the readers of this book will serve to reduce the number of divorces resulting from either spouse having Biblical grounds for divorce.

APPENDICES

One more clarification of Matthew 19:9

"And I say unto you, Whosoever shall put away his wife, except it be for fornication, and shall marry another, committeth adultery: and whoso marrieth her which is put away doth commit adultery."

We have already discussed in great detail that Jesus was not teaching that adultery was the only Biblical ground for divorce. After all, He, as God, is the one who commanded divorce for other grounds also in the Word of God. He was simply chastising the wicked men of Israel who were divorcing their wives because they were bored with them and wanted to move on to someone new.

There is another aspect of this verse, though, that also causes difficulty for some readers. It is understandable to most people why Jesus is telling the wicked husbands who have treacherously divorced their wives that they are committing adultery if they marry another wife afterward. What is not so easily understood, however, is the final part of the verse which reads, *"and whoso marrieth her which is put away doth commit adultery."* Since it was not the wife who was put away that did anything wrong, one might wonder why she would be prohibited from remarrying. The answer, though, is not so difficult as it may seem at first. Because God feels so strongly about the sanctity of marriage, and because the theoretical husband in the discussion had no Biblical grounds for putting away his wife, Jesus is saying that He still considers the original marriage to be in effect. From what we have already seen in other passages of the Mosaic Law, the wife clearly would have had Biblical grounds for divorce from her wicked husband had she wanted it; *but she is not the one who sought the divorce* in Jesus' example... it was the husband who had no Biblical grounds who sought the divorce. Therefore, the marriage, as far as God was concerned, was still in effect between the two. Nevertheless, as soon as the wicked husband married someone else (or had a one-night fling), his original wife would surely have then been free to marry since the wicked husband would have, in essence, committed adultery by beginning marital relations with someone new... which we already know would then give his original wife the liberty to marry someone new since she was no longer bound to the covenant.

Two times that divorce is explicitly prohibited in the Bible.

As we have seen, there are multiple instances in which the Bible says there exist legitimate grounds for divorce. On the other hand, however, there are only two instances in which divorce is explicitly prohibited; that is, there are two instances in which God said He would not allow a divorce no matter the situation or the desire of the person. The first of these instances we saw in the discussion of fraud when a husband accused his wife of having lied about being a virgin prior to their marriage. If she did, in fact, lie about this important matter, then the marriage covenant (contract) was a legal fraud and not enforceable by law. If, however, the husband was found to have fabricated the lie and claimed that she was not a virgin when, in fact, she was truly a virgin at the time of their wedding, the husband was to be beaten and fined... and was prohibited for the rest of his life from divorcing his wife. *"And the elders of that city shall take that man and chastise him; And they shall amerce him in an hundred shekels of silver, and give them unto the father of the damsel, because he hath brought up an evil name upon a virgin of Israel: and she shall be his wife; he may not put her away all his days"* (Deuteronomy 22:18,19). Later, in that same chapter, we find the second instance in which divorce is strictly prohibited. Verses 28 and 29 say, *"If a man find a damsel that is a virgin, which is not betrothed, and lay hold on her, and lie with her, and they be found; Then the man that lay with her shall give unto the damsel's father fifty shekels of silver, and she shall be his wife; because he hath humbled her, he may not put her away all his days."* This deals with a man who rapes a virgin. The law was that the perpetrator had to pay the girl's father a dowry... and then was prohibited from divorcing her for life even if he changed his mind about wanting to be with her for some reason later down the road. The purpose of this law was to provide a deterrent to any man who might think about raping a girl; he would be eliminating his own life choices from then on. One might ask, "How could anyone expect the girl to marry someone who had raped her?" The answer to that question is two-fold: 1) there is the possibility that she could be persuaded that the man who raped her genuinely was in love with her and not just "in lust," in which case she may wish to marry him; the prince of Shechem in Genesis was such a case with Jacob's daughter Dinah. 2) according to Jewish custom, the girl's father could choose to keep the dowry and not allow the man to marry his daughter, in which case the perpetrator was out the substantial sum of fifty shekels of silver... and still had no wife.

Divorce and remarriage

A question that arises more often than you might think is whether a husband and wife who have divorced each other and then married other people can divorce again and remarry their original spouses. I have known husbands and wives who have done this very thing. They divorced each other, and one or both of them married other people; then, the second marriages ended in divorce, and the original husband and wife came back together and remarried. This is lawful in most states even today; and many people who hear of such stories speak of them in glowing terms as though it were some romantic fairy tale. While it may be permitted in most states today, it is not permitted in God's Book. Deuteronomy 24:1-4 says, *"When a man hath taken a wife, and married her, and it come to pass that she find no favour in his eyes, because he hath found some uncleanness in her: then let him write her a bill of divorcement, and give it in her hand, and send her out of his house. And when she is departed out of his house, she may go and be another man's wife. And if the latter husband hate her, and write her a bill of divorcement, and giveth it in her hand, and sendeth her out of his house; or if the latter husband die, which took her to be his wife; Her former husband, which sent her away, may not take her again to be his wife, after that she is defiled; for that is abomination before the LORD:"* The reason that God does not permit such is because He views the marriage covenant seriously and divorce seriously. If a husband and wife follow through with their divorce and then marry other people, returning to their original spouses would make a mockery of the seriousness of both marriage and divorce; it would be tantamount to having an "open marriage" which has become so common among unbelievers in secular society in the last generation. This behaviour is no different than the animals of the field that come and go with whomever they please. God does not allow you to remarry your first spouse if either of you marry someone else in between. All husbands and wives should bear this in mind before making the final decision about ending their marriages in divorce.

With the prevalence of divorce in our society today, another question which arises more often than many might think is whether the marriage of someone who was unfaithful to his or her spouse, then divorced, and then married someone new is a legitimate marriage in the sight of God. Some have even gone so far as to ask if they should divorce their second spouses and remarry their original spouses once they realize that they were wrong to divorce in the first place. As we have just seen, God strictly prohibits remarrying the original spouse after having married someone else. What is equally important, however, is how God views the second marriage. Does He view the second marriage as legitimate even though the first marriage ended due to sin? We have a very clear answer to this question in the story of Jesus and the woman at the well found in the Gospel of John chapter 4. This woman was quite obviously an immoral woman. *"Jesus saith unto her, Go, call thy husband, and come hither. The woman answered and said, I have no husband. Jesus said unto her, Thou hast well said, I have no husband: For thou hast had five husbands; and he whom thou now hast is not thy husband: in that saidst thou truly."* It does not require a stretch of the imagination to assume that the reason this woman had been married and divorced five different times was owing to the fact that she had a problem staying at home and not running around with men outside of marriage. Yet surprisingly, Jesus referred to every single one of the men with whom she had had wedding ceremonies as her "husbands." He recognized each of them as a husband, not merely as illicit affairs. This demonstrates to us that while God clearly did not condone her behaviour that led to each of her divorces, once she was wed to someone else (even though it was likely the one with whom she had committed adultery), He still recognized the new marriage each time. God holds His institution of marriage in very high esteem, even when it is entered into by men and women of low morals. What can we take from this story in the Word of God? If you are presently in a marriage – even if it is with someone with whom you previously committed adultery while married to someone else – it is not God's desire for you to end your present marriage. Rather, He expects you to be faithful to whomever you are currently married... and He recognizes your marriage... so reform your life if necessary and make your present marriage one that honours Him.

Divorce and Qualifications of a Pastor

Paul's epistles to both Timothy and Titus speak of the qualifications of pastors and deacons, including the qualification of being *"the husband of one wife."*

There are several misconceptions about Paul's intention in this phrase, including the following:

Misconception #1) Pastors and church leaders must be married. Although there is a tendency in many conservative congregations to infer from this passage that a man must be married (and sometimes even have children, since the passage also says that he must rule his household well), this cannot be what Paul intended; for he clearly expressed the view that those serving the Lord at that time should remain unmarried - even as he was unmarried - if possible. In I Corinthians 7:8, Paul says "But I say to the unmarried and to widows that it is good for them if they remain even as I." Paul was clearly a leader in the New Testament church and, in fact, seems to have pastored the churches which he established on his missionary journeys until such time as he appointed men as pastors who had grown spiritually mature enough to serve in that role. Paul would not have stated that a man must be married in order to be an officer in the local church since he, himself, would have been disqualified if that were the case.

Misconception #2) Pastors and church leaders cannot be divorced, no matter the reason. The Bible gives a number of Scriptural grounds very explicitly stated for divorce. If a man has been divorced upon Biblical grounds, he is still clean and pure before the Lord, and, therefore, still qualified to hold the offices of both a pastor and a deacon. He is not disqualified Scripturally. Those who seek to disqualify such men are making judgments upon the same faulty logic as the Pharisees who had added their own traditions to the law in Jesus' day (Mark 7:1-13).

Literal exegesis of the Text:

The phrase "husband of one wife" in Greek is "mias gunaikos andra" which, literally rendered, means "a one-woman man."

"mias" = "only one"

"gunaikos" = "woman" (i.e. as in "gynocology")

"andra" = "man"

In the context of the qualifications of a bishop (pastor) or deacon, Paul is clearly teaching about the character required of a church leader. He is telling us that the man must be faithful, trustworthy, spiritually mature -- not a philanderer, not an adulterer, not promiscuous, not a fornicator, not someone who runs around on his wife, not one who divorces for unBiblical reasons and remarries. In short, he is someone who is faithful to God and to the Word of God... and hence to his wife (if he has one) as well.

Conclusion

1. A man does not have to be married to be a pastor or deacon, but he must be faithful if he is and morally pure even if he isn't.

2. If a man has been divorced, he must have had Biblical grounds for the divorce in order to remain "qualified" to serve as a pastor or deacon. He is not disqualified by the sins of someone else.

Made in the USA
Columbia, SC
25 May 2025

58273492R00091